untold

defining moments
of the uprooted

untold: defining moments of the uprooted

Copyedited by Mitali Desai
Cover illustration by Aishwarya Sukesh
Inner illustrations by Simran Sarin

For more information, please contact:
Mango & Marigold Press
Somerville, Massachusetts
hello@mangoandmarigoldpress.com

Library of Congress Control Number: 2020917210

CPSIA Code: PRV1120A
ISBN-13: 978-1-64543-716-1

Printed in the United States

*Dedicated to all the womxn who have been made
to feel like they were never enough—you are
and have always been more than enough.*

untold

defining moments
of the uprooted

edited by
Gabrielle Deonath and
Kamini Ramdeen

foreword by Tanuja Desai Hidier

CONTENTS

* Trigger warning: story includes sensitive material

FOREWORD

BY TANUJA DESAI HIDIER

FOR NEARLY TWO DECADES, the multicultural metropolis of London—where no one looks different among all the differences—had proven an apt and captivating home for my mixed-race family. After moving across the ocean at the turn of the millennium, I finally flew back to the States with my husband and our daughters in 2017. We had made this journey to Boston Logan Airport many times visiting before, but this time, we were moving back for good.

Prepping for our return, given the charged political climate on both sides of the pond, I was nervous about flying home—a first in my American-born brown girl life. Fortunately, our journey all the way to Wilbraham, Massachusetts, was wonderfully eventless.

Back in the Pioneer Valley, I was struck, as never before so consciously, by my old hometown's whiteness and small-town-suburbia silence. After so many years living away in big city melting pots, my brownness felt like a hullabaloo, an audiovisual disruption—a way it hadn't for a very long time.

I mulled over what had changed—and what had not—since I'd grown up here and since I'd left the U.S. From 9/11 to today's world.

And in the universe of my own family and friends. What was spoken in and around South Asian communities. And what was still untold.

So many of the issues at the core of this—race, religion, who may lay claim to a country or culture, the idea of home and belonging, who is given voice and granted space—had come to a painfully broader light after 9/11.

And here they were still, and are again.

People of color and of the diaspora have embodied these questions our whole lives long. So many of these battles are built into our very skin—where we are often encouraged to keep them, simmering, silent. And for brown womxn: an even more prevalent pressure to keep mum. Accommodate. Assimilate. Blend in, dumb down. Please. Not just vis a vis a dominant white world, but often within South Asian circuits as well, where much can be—and be encouraged to be—left unsaid.

But choosing silence is a risky business, especially when the voices given the vastest arena are those that would stifle the most vulnerable. Silence can scream volumes, thunderclap into complicity. And when borders, both physical and in the cultural psyche, wall us off from each other this way, we must respond with bridges—including the most potent bridge of all:

The saying of the unsaid.

The telling of our stories.

Since 2008, *Brown Girl Magazine* has made just this sort of storytelling—bringing the margins to the page—its trailblazing mission. Originating as a feminist platform for young South Asian womxn living in the U.S., *Brown Girl* has bloomed its audience across gender identities, age groups, and geographies, all the while honing its focus on embracing intersectionality, challenging cultural stigmas, deepening, and widening the definition of brownness—and breaking the silence.

Now, *Brown Girl*'s first anthology—*untold: defining moments of the uprooted*—compellingly continues this crucial conversation. This collection delves into the things—when it comes to identity, being, and relationships—we don't always talk about in mainstream society or South Asian circles. It tells, spells, some of these untolds—reflects some of the richness and complexity of our diaspora, the gifts and burdens that brown womxn carry today.

Penned by thirty-two emerging voices with contributions from American, British, Canadian, and Indo-Caribbean communities, these intergenerational creative nonfiction pieces span from Pakistan to Guyana, from hair salons to hospitals, art and heart to hearth and home. With stories centering immigration, infertility, caste, coming out, marriage, mental health, domestic violence, parenting our children and our elderly, grief, self-belief, and the journey to self-love, *untold* honors our watershed moments.

And relays the tale of a boundless community.

These chronicles are universal. And yet: Each, unique. Because brown itself is an infinite identity. And being a brown womxn is an ever-evolving, layered experience.

As it has always been. But cultural hubs and havens like *Brown Girl Magazine*—such vital community keys—were once nowhere to be seen.

These Massachusetts streets I paced after my return to the States were ones I'd wandered as a child, imagining stories night and day, dreaming of being a writer. However, at that time no cultural mirrors and windows were to be found: no people of our particular diasporic background visible, audible, or reachable on TV, in bands, in magazines, on bookshelves, nor on these same lanes and drives. And so, there were none even in my imagination.

Over many years, that lack—that untold—would begin to take on the shape and weight and intricacy of a story. And in my telling of it, so many undiscussed memories would surface decades after the fact: my father, eating khichdi kadhi with his hands, switching abruptly to the cutlery my mother would whisk his way, in a silent diaspora dance of shame, were someone to appear at the door; my being deemed the color of dog poo at recess, accused of witchcraft and spell-casting, sand flung in my five-year-old eyes.

Brownness was a complicated experience outside of this whitewashed world too. I first realized I was of the diaspora, and not considered *Indian* Indian, only when I got to university and heard the term ABCD—American Born Confused Desi—directed at me by my first South Asian (born and raised) friends. My reaction was excitement that there was a term for us in-betweeners at all. But I also wondered:

Shouldn't we be naming ourselves?

It wasn't until my mid-twenties that I began applying this lightbulb moment to my own writing. That change came not from within but from a fellow workshopper in a creative writing class at the Writer's Voice in New York City who asked why my heroine was white when her point of view was so clearly from another vantage point. Another student cut to the chase:

"Why don't you just make her Indian?"

They were proven right by a few strokes of Find/Replace, with nearly no other revision required. Amy from Minneapolis became Indian-American East Coast Kayla. Suddenly, I was writing a collection of connected brown girl short stories. Perhaps even a book?

Suddenly, it all hung together!

And then promptly unraveled. I just didn't feel Indian enough to write the Indian parts of this project, nor American enough to write the American. One night out, I was lamenting this fact to a Croatian-

American writer friend when she looked at me, nodded thoughtfully, and said:

"Maybe *that's* your story."

It turned out to be a milestone moment in my journey toward finding my voice. The idea that this feeling of being *not enough* was actually *more than.* That this neither-here-nor-there identity was, in fact, a You Are Here.

That the untold could *be* the story.

And what became clear to me later, as I told my own untolds through my fiction—and what is crystalline today, in reading those included here—is:

We don't have to squeeze ourselves into some box; we don't have to fit in *at all.* There's nothing to fit *into.* We're beyond labels. Roomier than either/or. More ample than us/them. We're *and/and.*

Yes. Being brown—being a brown womxn—is *and/and.*

Telling our stories is a form of resistance: to the status quo, being stereotyped, split in two, sidelined, silenced. It is also persistence: a making and taking up of space. And it is insistence. That someone hear—*needs* to hear—what we have to say. Insistence on honoring our moments, our "maybe *that's* your story" moments.

Moments that, when strung together, are *momentous.*

Moments that reveal, bone by breath, the beating heart of a life, that launch us into *new* lives. Land us into ourselves.

 Growing up, if I could have imagined such an anthology could exist, this celebration of our browns in their abundance; if my parents could have held this book in hand during those lonely first American Dream days...

Well, now we can.

So now. Today. What has changed?

Now, today, the stories I am thinking about are our own. And "our own" is a more expansive, inclusive, resplendent space.

And now, right here, in these pages, we share some of this manifold medley of the South Asian experience. We reveal and revel in our multidimensional selves. By bringing all the browns we embody—in all their beauty, all their bounty—to the tale.

So thank you to the brave brown womxn who dug deeper—through the silence and into sound. Poured their own ink from brown hands to book page to turn it many-hued. And thank you to all of you reading, all of you out there in the world, molding, making it, too—by seeking, speaking *your* truths.

The city we live as brown womxn, as humans, is *multiplicity*.

A hyphen doesn't have to be a border. It can also be a bridge.

Never underestimate the power of your own voice. Use it.

Stories save lives. Y(ours) included.

You, we, are not alone. Our words can lift us. Roots can grow.

And our untolds *are* stories...simply waiting to be known.

INTRODUCTION

BY TRISHA SAKHUJA-WALIA

TWO WEEKS BEFORE MY FIRST DAY OF SCHOOL IN
AMERICA, we landed in Queens, New York—America's melting pot.
Papa was sponsored by his company in Bhopal, India, to go to New
York City on a three-year work visa. With a handful of degrees under
my parents' belts, a five-year-old and eleven-month-old, and a few
suitcases with our most prized possessions, we anxiously left our
motherland for a once-in-a-lifetime opportunity.

In May 1995, I found out that nothing is more isolating than
being the new kid at school in a foreign country. I only had a few
English words under my belt—tooth fairy, train, airplane—and I
embarrassingly learned the hard way that teachers in America were
not called "madame." I became the shy kid in class who would only
speak when called on.

My parents thought we'd assimilate into the American way of life
easily. But instead, we stuck out—just like my steel tiffin did on the
first day of school among identical plastic lunch trays of peanut butter
and jelly sandwiches. I distinctly remember putting my homemade
lunch—one roti, fried lady's finger with mango achaar on the side,

and a small caramel-flavored toffee—back in my bookbag before my classmates could make fun of me or notice my lack of Americanness.

"What tribe are you from?" a student in class once asked me.

He mistakenly thought I was the "Indian" he was reading about in his textbook during social studies.

"I'm not from a tribe. I'm from India," I said sheepishly, unable to muster the courage to say more.

From then on, I dodged questions about where I was from, tried to enjoy peanut butter and jelly sandwiches and pizza for lunch, attempted to play softball, joined the swim team at the YMCA, took karate classes, listened to The Spice Girls, watched *Space Jam* and *Arthur*, and dressed up for Halloween as a ninja turtle. These were just some of the foundational building blocks of my newfound American identity. On the flip side, I tried my best to forget about everything that made me Indian—so much so that I forgot my mother tongue. Soon, Hindi became foreign, Madhuri Dixit's dance sequences were replaced by James Bond action shots, and the Backstreet Boys poster I found inside my Cheerios opened up my eyes to a whole new world.

I spent a lot of my younger years pretending because I so badly wanted to fit in. But in my twenties, questions that had been bubbling below the surface became harder to ignore: *Why was I constantly trying to choose one part of my identity over the other? Why can't I embrace both?* I became hell-bent on making a space for my two worlds to co-exist. This quest fueled my desire and need for *Brown Girl Magazine* to exist, and it manifested itself into something far beyond the borders of my imagination.

Born out of the lack of South Asian representation in mainstream media, *Brown Girl Magazine* was created by diasporic womxn who believe in the power of storytelling as a vehicle for community building and empowerment. What began as a passion project I stumbled upon in college is now a full-time venture with hundreds of dedicated contributors paving the way for the next generation of storytellers. On this platform, womxn like me never have to hide, pretend, be shy, or dismiss who they are. And, after more than a decade of establishing this space online, we wanted to expand our mission to the world of print.

In January 2019, we began the journey of curating *Brown Girl's* first-ever anthology. Wanting to include diverse emerging voices from all corners of the world, we put out an open call for story pitches and received more than 150 submissions. Each one was pored over with immense gratitude, and throughout the next year, we whittled that pool down to the thirty-one deeply personal stories you are about to read.

Each piece, told through a creative nonfiction lens, explores a defining moment in the lives of these writers. They touch on topics that, in the larger South Asian community, are usually left *untold*. This common thread inherent throughout each of the following stories— the willingness to delve into the buried parts of this experience—led us to this title.

Written by an intergenerational group of South Asian contemporary storytellers from the U.S., U.K., and Canada, these pieces shed light on the realities faced by those living in the diaspora today, where there is often a shared feeling of not belonging here—in the lands we've come to know as home—nor there—where all of our roots were first planted.

In three sections, each author brings an uprooted view to the themes of identity, being, and relationships.

Identity explores the ways in which others perceive us and how we define ourselves. These narratives of self-discovery and reflection take us down the winding roads of immigration, racism, coming out, caste, faith, living in a post-9/11 world, and conformity or lack thereof.

In *Being*, we probe the many parts of our existence—from body to mind to soul. In this examination of South Asian womxn's journeys, we expose the harsh truths of colorism, womxn's health, mental health, suicide, addiction, infertility, and connection to body.

Relationships highlight the essential bonds that shape us, mold us, bring joy, and wreak havoc in our lives. These moments give a glimpse into the sometimes-precarious roles that womxn play as lovers, wives, mothers, sisters, daughters, daughters-in-law, and best friends.

Throughout the process of curating this collection, we've made a number of intentional choices. In picking the creative nonfiction writing style, we wanted to give readers the most authentic look into these life-changing moments by encouraging writers to employ the elements of dialogue, sensory wording, and imagery. In order to accomplish this to the fullest extent, we edited these stories countless times and pushed writers to dig deeper and unveil their truths in the most unadulterated way—the result is a testament to their courage and bravery in giving voice to their most personal untold moments.

Another purposeful decision we've held strong throughout the editing process is not italicizing words in different languages and dialects. For too long, the words of our community—and other minority communities—have been othered, watered down, and over-explained. In this anthology, we are normalizing the parts of our hyphenated identities that are considered foreign in Western societies.

For generations, we have hidden behind the societal expectations and obligations of those before us. Too scared to speak our truth, too afraid to be seen for who we are, or too proud to admit our wrongs, but *Brown Girl* has served as a space to do the opposite. While no one book can give a 360-degree view of South Asian diasporic experiences, this anthology offers you a window into thirty-two of the infinite sides that make up this cultural phenomenon.

It is a hopeful start to the telling of all the untolds we hold within but desperately want to let out.

identity

~~Brwn Grl~~
Brown Girl

COMING OUT AGAIN (AND AGAIN)

BY RITA SENGUPTA

"MOM, KELLY AND I ARE DATING."

It was the second time in my life I told my mom I was dating a woman. The Oklahoma summer sun crept higher in the sky as we sat in the backyard of my childhood home. After a long, piercing moment of silence, I asked,

"Is there anything you want to say?"

She nodded in the same way she moved her head in agreement with a pastor's Sunday sermon.

"I'll be praying for you both," she said.

I already knew the answer, but I asked anyway.

"What exactly will you be praying for, Mom?" I took a sip of my now cold cup of chai.

"That one day, you two will find godly men," she said, looking directly at me.

The first time she told me about this prayer was when I came out to her three years prior, so I was not shocked by her response.

In the South Asian community, my family is a bit of a rarity. My dad is a Hindu Bengali-Indian, mostly secular, and my mom is a Punjabi-Pakistani and a devout Christian, another rarity in itself.

Growing up in an interfaith household, my parents never forced either religion on me or my brother. Attending a Sunday morning church service was usually followed by an afternoon puja at the temple to equalize our religious exposure. Despite their seeming laissez-faire attitude on our Sunday activities, my mom's steadfast faith overpowered my dad's apathy for organized religion. It's hard not to get Jesus-is-the-reason-for-the-season vibes when you step into our house. There are end tables accompanied with religious novels, note cards with handwritten Bible verses strewn about the kitchen counter, and Christian hymns in Urdu bursting out of a speaker.

Anytime I have something going on in my life—an upcoming audition, a big show, a cold—my mom is always there with a prayer: "I'll be praying for you, mere paro. Love and blessings to you, and the Lord bless you always abundantly!"

When I first came out to her, I nervously told her through many tears that I was attracted to women. She immediately affirmed that she loved me very much but then reiterated her divine request for God to send me a Matthew, Mark, Luke, or John.

She didn't completely dismiss me from her life, however. Most coming out scenes I saw on TV ended in two scenarios—complete rejection or complete acceptance. What happens when your religious mom loves you *and* is also simultaneously praying that Kirk Cameron will be her future son-in-law? I concluded that her reaction wasn't as bad as it could've been and assumed my coming out process was finished.

But on that summer morning when I told my mom about Kelly, I felt like I was coming out all over again. It was discouraging that even when I had found comfort in who I was and found someone whom I loved, her mission to pray the gay away was as unrelenting as ever.

"Well, let's just agree to disagree," I said, knowing there was no way I could convince her to become a rainbow ally and there was no way she could convince me to become a born-again Jesus devotee. While the two aren't morally equivalent, *How could I ask her to change who she was?* I thought. *How could she ask me the same?*

She agreed to disagree.

"What do you want to eat for lunch?" she asked without missing a beat, as if we didn't just have an hour-long dispute.

What do you want to eat—the quintessential non-sequitur for South Asian parents after an argument.

We went to the kitchen and warmed up leftover keema and roti.

A few years following that conversation with my mom, my relationship with Kelly started to progress. We had moved to New York City with our boxer-pitbull mix, George, and started to establish our life in a cozy Brooklyn apartment. I felt comfortable telling my mom that we moved in together. Living with an unmarried partner is taboo in our culture because it can lead to having a child out of wedlock. Birth control, thankfully, is part of the benefits package of a same-sex relationship.

She didn't express her opposition to our one-bedroom situation. She didn't even reiterate her prayer for us to find godly men. Instead, on our weekly catch-up call, she would either change the subject or ignore my comment altogether if I mentioned Kelly's name. *If she doesn't acknowledge our relationship, then maybe she thinks it will eventually disappear*, I thought. I grew accustomed to my mom's disregard for my sexual identity. Avoiding conflict was easier than habitually re-establishing my queerness.

The years of sweeping my grievances under the rug had made my life very dusty. I started to envy my straight friends who brought their boyfriends home for the holidays. On family vacations, seeing my brother and his wife made me miss Kelly, who I didn't invite because I didn't want to make my mom uncomfortable.

Pretending that my very gay, very long-term girlfriend was nonexistent was, well, very exhausting. My relationship with Kelly was not an experimental phase like that one time I decided to be vegetarian for two weeks. I realized I had to give up my habit of avoiding conflict. I needed to be firm with my mom about my identity. I needed to come out—again.

I decided the best way to establish the seriousness of my relationship was to bring Kelly with me on a trip home to Oklahoma City. I'd always wanted to show her where I grew up, and my need to normalize us was now a priority. I anxiously called my mom and asked if Kelly could visit. Her answer was resolute.

"No," she said, with even more intensity than when she told me she would pray for me.

My mom would not allow Kelly to stay in the house. I tried to reason with her for as long as I could, hoping to change her mind somehow. Still, she wouldn't budge, and I was left weary and defeated.

After that intense phone call, we spoke only a handful of times for the next year and a half. We sent each other birthday texts. I once sent her a picture of my failed attempt at making roti, and she texted back, `Nice mere paro`, and closed it with her classic phrase, `love and blessings always abundantly`. After a while, our texts grew further apart. Months went by and I didn't hear from her.

The result of that conversation was harder than coming out

to her the first and second times combined. My mom had been my constant cheerleader my entire life, supporting my every decision and believing I could do whatever and be whoever I wanted—but my relationship with a woman was the one thing she could not rally behind. Therapy, a supportive girlfriend, and many slices of Tony's Pizza grounded me during this time. But on most days, it was easy to let the negative emotions take over as I mindlessly clicked next episode after hours of Netflix binging.

After a half dozen unanswered texts and calls to my mom, I stopped trying. I didn't have the energy to keep coming out, but I never closed the door on our relationship. I knew I couldn't rush or force my mom to come to a place of acceptance sooner than she was ready to.

Then one day, it happened. My mom called me. Our conversation was punctuated with long silences, but our love for each other loudly filled the air. I don't know what happened to spark the call—and I'm not sure I'll ever know why—but there was a shift in our relationship.

A few weeks after she called, my mom and dad came to visit us in New York. It was as if the past year and a half was a bad dream that I had just woken up from. My mom and Kelly laughed with each other, arm in arm, as we walked and ate all over Brooklyn. The two of them were getting along so well; I was even a little jealous. I wondered if I should remind my mom that Kelly was a raging homosexual. At the end of the weekend, she gifted Kelly a leather-bound, engraved Holy Bible.

At first, I felt like my mom had *Punk'd* us. After a lovely weekend, the Bible came across as an unsolicited reminder of my mom's original prayer to find us God-fearing husbands. But the gift could have been just a good-natured Christian gesture.

Either way, I take it for what it is and wonder if I'll have to come out to her—again.

PERFORMING LINES

BY L.M. IYER

THOUGH I TRIED TO APPEAR CONFIDENT, I couldn't help but sway slightly in front of the audience in the terrace room. I had performed many times before to the point that I'd boiled it down to a science: I would sign up for local open mics, write different versions of the same piece about race and mental health and beauty and gender, perform it in what I called my hot girl costume—a tiny bralette, fishnet tights, and combat boots—and wait to soak in the validation that would inevitably follow. People would come up to me afterward and say how much they liked my work, how relatable and resonant and powerfully vulnerable I was, and I'd smile back and thank them, feeling like I deserved both the world and nothing at all.

Tonight's piece was especially provocative. I had written about my experience growing up in upper-crust suburbia and titled it "A Multi-Step Guide to Whitewashing." The same clichés showed up in all my work: detachment from Indian and American culture alike, body size, insecurity, depression, and changing myself to be appreciated, noticed, desired by someone—anyone. But this time, I made sure to highlight that I was self-aware, that I was not a victim.

"I know what I'm doing," I told the audience, my voice clear, even, and a touch too loud. "It hasn't been unconscious."

I called myself out for performing authenticity at the same time as I performed my authenticity. I fell into performing a few years earlier as I embarked on a journey of extreme self-transformation. After losing too much weight, I went to speak to a psychiatrist. In one of our sessions in his narrow office, we somehow approached the topic of race. I told him that I had never fit in because I was so much darker, so visibly different from everyone else.

"Do you think that's why you changed your body? Because you couldn't change your skin?" he asked, peering at me over his glasses.

Growing up, I was one of the only non-white girls in my hometown, and the members of my family were the only South Asians for miles around. I tried my hardest to assimilate into whiteness, denouncing my language, religion, and culture. All I wanted was to be like the people around me, inside and out. I played a game with myself in the shower every day, gripping my fleshy stomach with chewed nails, pretending I had wishes that I could spend on lightening my skin and shrinking every extra inch on my body that took up too much undeserved space.

Even though I tried to blend in, my dark skin combined with an ethnic name immediately marked me as *other*. My peers made fun of my body shape, laughed at how I walked and spoke, and called me a terrorist behind my back. I learned that my appearance set the tone for how others treated me, and I grew to hate how I looked because I didn't feel it was an accurate reflection of who I was. I felt like there was some other kind of essence inside of me, something pure and white, caged within walls of brown flesh. I wanted to take this essence out of myself and put her in a lithe, pale body, so she would be allowed to navigate the world freely and without reproach. I couldn't even get angry at my peers for making fun of my appearance because I felt it wasn't truly mine.

When I went off to college, I didn't just want to let go of who I was before. I wanted to annihilate her. I'd been called fat, so I lost fifty pounds. I'd been called unattractive, so I began dating everyone I could, collecting partners like baseball cards. I rarely ever looked at them—I only thought about how they looked at me. I developed a penchant for fashion, adorning my newly slender frame with short skirts, thigh-high boots, and strappy bras. Changing my appearance and watching people's reactions became an addiction, and I was always chasing my next hit. I was looking for anything to make up for my brownness, finding footholds wherever I could to gain positive attention, even if only for a moment.

However, in my new environment, I promptly realized that I was no longer too brown but now too white. My college was in a highly diverse area, and other South Asians—whom I referred to as "people who looked like me" because it felt looser and more comfortable—seemed so far removed. I joined a South Asian student group to get used to being around other brown people because that's what I was after all, but I could barely hold a conversation with them. I'd never even seen a Bollywood movie. The whiteness that I'd forced upon myself growing up had become a hindrance, and I was left without any community that truly understood me. Brown classmates would talk about their heritage, their background:

"I'm from Kerala."

"I'm Malayali."

"It's such a Punjabi stereotype, you know?"

I would laugh along.

"Yeah, for sure," I would say, even though it all seemed the same to me.

I had spent my life on the borders, the in-betweens, the gap between how I saw myself and how everyone else saw me—too brown for white people and too white for brown people—when all I wanted was somewhere I belonged, where I knew exactly who I should be.

"You exhibit a lot of black-and-white thinking," the psychiatrist said.

"Of course I do," I replied. "That's the only way I know anything. That's the only way I can figure out where I'm supposed to go."

I tried to drown out this feeling of unbelonging, but I couldn't. Instead, I turned to exploiting myself and my story: sex and tragedy sold, so I combined the two, packaged them, and made them into a show.

Back in the terrace room, I finished my piece, concluding with a line on self-assimilation:

"The only way you win is by losing."

I gazed out into the audience through thickly lined eyes, straightened my shoulders, and fought the urge to rub my clavicles. At this point, my bones had become my most faithful totem. Touching them made me feel real, reminding me that this was my body, solidly mine—even if it didn't always feel like it. It wasn't that I loved this costume, but I depended on it. The sexy, magnetic, tragic performer.

"Thank you," I said quickly, ducking my head and stepping off stage. A beat passed before the applause started, soft and then stronger as my words sunk in.

That's the key to a good performance—to leave everyone wanting more before they look at you long enough to see everything you're trying to hide.

THE HAIR CUT

BY RAVLEEN K.

THE SALON WAS THE SIZE OF A SMALL WALK-IN CLOSET. Girls who looked like they were barely out of high school hovered over the chairs, learning how to thread and tweeze eyebrows, upper lips, and chins. Haircutting had recently popped up as a popular service in the Sikh-dominated region of Punjab, to where my family and I had traveled a long twenty-two hours from Louisiana for a wedding.

The sun was setting, and the hairstylist was about to go home when my mother, cousin, and I arrived slightly late for my first-ever hair appointment. The stylist was clearly irritated with our tardiness, but he was forced to stay by his mom, the parlor owner.

"Remember, Sania, when you came two hours late and the baraat already reached my house? We're allowed to be late now to make up for that," my mom said.

They both laughed while Sania pestered her son to set up his station again.

"Mumma!" he groaned, half his tools already packed into his black box.

"Listen to me," Sania said with a hiss.

25

Looking at me, she nodded toward the stylist's chair.

"Sit, beta. He'll take care of you," she said, rolling her eyes at her son.

I sat in the chair as he lazily draped a black smock over my clothes. My oiled knee-length hair tied in a loose braid cascaded over my back. I was shaking with excitement. I had been planning this haircut for weeks before we arrived in India, googling pictures of different types of cuts. From feathered ends to blunt fringes, the possibilities were endless.

"So, I was thinking about layers and a V-shape cut with long bangs in the front. I don't want it kept too long—you should be able to tell I got a haircut," I told the hairdresser, eagerly. "I want my hair parted on the right side. I don't like straight parts. Do we have to re-part and re-braid my hair for that? Should I take my hair out of the braid? Are you going to wash it first?"

As he got to work, my mom went from laughing about her wedding day with Sania to shaking on a stool in the small corner facing my salon chair. Her bottom lip began to tremble, and she covered her face with her hand, peeping through her fingers to look at me. The parlor wali looked nervous as he took my hair—which I had never cut once in all my thirteen years—in his hand. He sloppily chopped into my braid, and with one quick snip, nearly half of it was gone. My mom gasped for air between her sobs as the stylist sheepishly handed her the cut stands, which she quickly tucked into a black plastic bag. He was from a Hindu family in the city and was clearly puzzled by my mom's heaving and crying.

Before arriving at the parlor, my mom told me that when a Sikh cuts their hair, they either keep the cut hair stowed away safely or throw it into a river. She gathered herself and watched the hairstylist snip away every last piece of my religious identity. I left the parlor feeling relieved. My head and heart both felt light as I hopped into the car to ride back to our village. I thought to myself, *Wow, I finally get to fit in. People are finally going to like me.*

Back home in Louisiana, I stood in front of my dresser in my dimly lit room. The sun had barely risen, but I had forced myself out of bed an extra hour early to get ready for school. I was excited to debut my new look. Everything had to be perfect. My mom had ironed my uniform khakis the night before, my white shirt was freshly washed, and I had a brand-new pair of black-and-white Converse sneakers calling my name. Since my big chop, I had learned that my natural hair was actually quite curly and dry, and using the thin-toothed comb my mom picked up from the bazaar in Punjab wasn't doing my curls any favors. I found a wide-toothed comb instead and carefully ran it through my hair, unknotting it layer by layer. I took the extra precaution of tapering down any flyaways with a toothbrush and topped off the whole look with a generous amount of hair spray to make sure it all stayed in place.

My new hair has to look perfect and effortless, just like the other girls at school, I thought.

As I finished styling my hair, I thought about how all my worries were about to vanish. Every morning, I went to school on edge, waiting for cruel comments from my classmates. I was never sure who was going to make a comment about my hair or crack a terrorist joke in front of the class. I'd usually walk from class to class with my head down, holding my breath, hoping no one would single me out with their taunts.

Sometimes Danny, the half-Korean kid, would make a spectacle out of me. I'd look in his direction innocently while walking to the cafeteria, and he'd spit at me.

"What're you looking at, hairy dothead?"

I'd look away in shame while kids around me perked up hearing the taunts, but his insults didn't stop there.

"You're related to Osama, aren't you? You kinda look like him."

I didn't have the courage to say anything back—when I did, it only fueled his fire.

"Who do you think you are, talking back to me? Aren't your people poor slaves in India? Shut up, bitch."

I couldn't answer his questions or reason with him. Every time, he just took my words and made new insults out of them. And the last thing I wanted to do was fight his bullying with more bullying. I could have just as easily made racist remarks about him being Korean, but then I thought, *How would that make me any better?* So I kept my mouth shut in quiet solidarity for the Asian in him. He was the accepted minority in rural Louisiana: non-threatening and light-skinned.

Danny's bullying was awful, but middle school girls—as I came to find out—were way worse. P.E. was an especially difficult class to deal with; every time I moved, my long braid moved with me, whipping through the air violently. When I was in the seventh grade, brand new to middle school and unaware we'd be required to wear shorts as part of the gym uniform, I showed up to class completely unshaved. I never quite lived down the embarrassment I felt walking out of the locker room with a garden on my legs. It took a while, but my mom finally let me shave my legs during the following summer.

In eighth grade, before P.E. class started, we sat on the polished gym floor in neat rows in alphabetical order. There were five rows with six girls each, and I ended up sitting next to this seemingly sweet girl, April. Every day, I'd plop down next to her at P.E.

"Hi, Ravleen," she'd say in her high-pitched voice.

Other days, she'd smile at me as we walked past each other in the locker room or share her hair ties with me when mine broke. I quickly learned that she was actually quite vicious. While waiting for the coach to assign us into teams, I was re-braiding my hair tighter in preparation for our unit about volleyball.

April leaned over from the row next to me.

"Your hair looks like a piece of shit growing out of your head. How do you use the bathroom like that?" she said, her face showing no sign of emotion.

I was stunned and speechless. This girl had been so nice and kind to me up until today. I heard snickering and knew some of the other girls had heard my P.E. buddy turn on me.

How do you even respond to that? I looked away, too embarrassed to react.

The worst bullying, though, came from Carrie and Alexis. They wouldn't insult me in the hallways where people were just passing by or in the gym where the coaches and other students couldn't always hear over the sounds of basketballs and squeaking shoes. They came for me in a classroom of over twenty-five students in the middle of lectures and presentations, distracting me from learning. The bullying was usually done behind the teacher's back, with Carrie looking me up and down and then whispering something to Alexis, who would then pass the nasty comments across the classroom like a game of telephone. It was always about my hair.

"What's the point?"

"Does she even wash it?"

"What's it like peeing with it?"

"Why doesn't she just cut her hair?"

"I wonder what she would do if someone just cut it?"

Sometimes, the teachers—who were supposed to protect their students or at the very least be neutral parties—took part in the bullying.

We were split into groups of four or five to work on a set of algebra worksheets for the class period.

"She's going to India to see her Uncle Osama. And then she's going to come back with that disease on her hands," my classmate Hunter whispered to our group. I stared down at my work, trying to ignore what Hunter said, but everyone who overheard him snickered, even the other groups. The "disease" he was talking about was mehndi. My algebra partner Lenny leaned over and said,

"Damn, you got some bushy brows. Can you grow them long like your hair?"

At that moment, I lost it. I was fuming and couldn't think of who to go to for help. I shot out of my seat and made eye contact with our math teacher, Mr. Landry. Confused at my sudden movements, he nodded at me to speak.

"He said I'm going to India to see my Uncle Osama. I'm not from a terrorist family," I said loudly, pointing at Hunter. Hunter looked at the teacher innocently with his big brown eyes. He was barely five feet and seemed like an innocent little puppy compared to my five-foot-seven-inch frame.

Instead of scolding Hunter or asking him to stop, Mr. Landry burst into laughter. His pale face turned red while he gasped for breath in between giggles. I sat down in shock and slouched in my seat. It felt like the yellow walls of the classroom were closing in on me. My eyes welled up as I hung my head in shame and cried into my worksheet. I wasn't safe from anyone—not even my teachers.

~&

As the sun rose and my mom fumbled around the kitchen packing my lunch for the school day, I experimented with my hair. *Should I do a deep part or something in the center?* I settled on center-right, so it wouldn't look dramatic. I wasn't used to having bangs hanging over my forehead anyway. Then I moved my hair over my left shoulder, the same way I would wear my braid to protect it from getting chopped off in a sneak attack from someone behind me. *But what if I split it and had it on both sides of my face? What if I just threw it back so the chop would be more subtle?* I pondered a bit and decided that it wouldn't make a difference. The long braid was gone, and even if I threw it into a ponytail, everyone would notice the three feet of hair missing.

I emerged from my room, new shoes perfectly double-knotted and every strand of hair in place. I grabbed my lunchbox, stuffed it into my backpack, and kissed my mom goodbye before skipping to the bus stop. I waited eagerly for the bus as the sticky air began to frizz my curls. Not wanting to ruin my new, polished look, I gathered the hair and tucked it inside my sweater, the same way I had seen my classmates do. The hair on my scalp would be frizzy, but at least the big curls would be safe. When the bus arrived, I plopped down in the first seat behind my bus driver, Ms. Kelsey, who didn't seem to notice anything amiss with me. I quietly watched out the window as we picked up more kids from each neighborhood and made our way to the busy town center where our middle school was located.

When we arrived at school, I hopped off the bus and dramatically pulled my curly locks out of the sweater, flipping my hair up and out with both hands. My friend Hannah was getting off her bus behind mine at the same time. She saw my new hair and audibly gasped. She ran up to me, her dirty blonde waves bouncing and big eyes lit up with excitement.

"Ravleeeen! You cut your hair. Now that new boy in class might actually like you."

Before I could even respond, she grabbed me by the hand and whisked me away to the stairs while she went on about Brandon, the new kid in the same math class my teacher had insulted me in. I couldn't focus on Hannah updating me on the gossip I had missed while I was in India.

"Brandon has the same skin color as you. He's not super pale. You might have a shot," she droned on. "Also, Mr. Landry changed our seating chart. I think he moved you away from Hunter, but Brandon isn't far from you. All the girls think he's cute."

All I could think about was what she had said—that my long hair had made me undesirable.

As we climbed the stairs to the second floor, everyone around me stared. There were some hushed whispers while others glanced at me in shock and looked away when they noticed my gaze. I began to feel uncomfortable. *Why do they look mad?* I thought to myself. I pulled open the heavy doors and marched down the dim hallway to my homeroom. I took a deep breath before entering the classroom, knowing this moment would symbolize a new beginning for me. I stepped in and immediately looked everyone in the front row in the eyes. I slowly walked across the room to my desk in the far corner. Everyone was quiet and seemed to stare at my every move until I sat down.

Danny was wide-eyed and silent. *I bet you weren't expecting this, huh?* I thought to myself, regaining some confidence and pride. Sitting behind Danny, Alexis and Carrie spoke to each other slyly with their eyes. Alexis shuffled over to my desk as Carrie, Danny, and my other classmates watched. She stood in front of me as she combed her fingers through her caramel-brown hair and stared at me with blank, icy eyes. She cocked her head to the side. Her hair fell perfectly at the middle of her chest with the ends slightly flipped inward.

"Girl, your hair is even shorter than mine now. I miss your long hair," she said with a smile before flipping her hair in my face.

As I watched her stomp back to her seat, I thought of the frayed strands that my mother had sadly tucked into that small plastic bag. And suddenly, I missed it too.

ANYWHERE BUT INDIA

BY SHARDA SEKARAN

MY MOTHER WRANGLED YARDS of delicate fabric and beads with her hands. We were attempting to wrap a golden yellow sari around my body—something neither of us had ever done before and most reasonable people probably wouldn't attempt for the first time on their wedding day. I was in Copenhagen, Denmark, far away from anyone I knew who could help us. I consulted friends via group chats, messages, and video calls. I studied YouTube and crossed my fingers, literally, over and over again, trying to achieve proper pleats.

I felt in my soul that I should wear the sari. This gesture was a part of my choice to show up as my whole self for this new chapter in life.

But my wedding day wasn't an elaborate affair. *It's a small city hall ceremony with only our most immediate family and a handful of local friends*, I thought. *I could still chicken out at the last minute and show up in whatever attire I want, if need be.*

❧

About a decade earlier, I tried to go to India for the first time in my life, but I never made it further than the Atlanta airport. I'd stuffed everything I could into the purple backpack that had taken me across Europe, Latin America, and Africa. It still smelled vaguely of dust from a past journey. This was supposed to be my first visit to the homeland of my father, a man I'd never known. All he had given me was his physical features, my name, and a long thread of unanswered questions woven throughout my life.

I had no family to welcome me to India, only the invitation of a friend to join her on a trip through Rajasthan. She was of South Asian descent and had been to India many times. She brimmed with enthusiasm and seemed unphased by the vagueness of my plans. I told her I wanted to part ways at some point in the journey so I could make my way south to Tamil Nadu to see what I could learn about my origins. She was unaware that I was carrying decades of anguish along with my purple backpack.

When I arrived at the airport, I found out that my flight was delayed. I was warned that I might miss my connection and arrive a day late. The likely outcome was that I would not arrive in Delhi in time to meet up with my friend and her travel companions. I could find a way to catch up with them, but I would have to negotiate the start of the journey on my own. An airline staffer apologized for the inconvenience and told me that, because I'd booked the ticket with frequent flyer miles, I had the option of canceling and reclaiming those miles without any penalty.

I stood there alone at the service desk, saddled with my overstuffed backpack. I hadn't checked a bag. I could bail on this whole endeavor without any consequence. I thought about my life and my wildly ambivalent feelings about India. There was too much gravity, too much emotion. The risk of having a bad experience felt like more than I could bear. I took this unexpected eject button as a cosmic sign. I gathered myself and left the airport.

My father was Tamil but was born and raised in Bombay. He met my mother in the 1970s while studying as an international graduate student at Michigan State University. She was African American, had grown up in Detroit, and was the first in her family to go to college. It was probably the first time in my father's life that he'd been so far from home and beyond the confines imposed by his family's gaze.

My mother, on the other hand, was geographically close to home but was a whole world away from the life she'd known when it came to race, culture, and class. She was from a close-knit community where the boundaries of possibility scarcely extended beyond her immediate neighborhood. She had an interest in photography and met my father after spotting him on campus. She'd never seen a person who looked quite like him—with his dark brown skin and long black hair—and asked to take his picture. In turn, he asked to take her photo, and a romance emerged.

As their relationship progressed, she noticed that he was strangely secretive about it, careful to keep her away from his colleagues and friends. Nonetheless, they moved in together and got married, also in a no-fuss city hall ceremony with even fewer people in attendance than mine. My father completed his PhD at the University of Michigan in Ann Arbor, where I was born. Not long after, when I was still a baby, he accepted a job offer in Chicago. He told my mother that he would set things up and send for us later.

But he never did. He just left.

I filled in the blanks of his absence based on my mother's accounts. She said he had told her that he was under pressure from his traditional Brahmin family to marry someone of their choosing, and his parents threatened to commit suicide if he disobeyed. They would have never accepted a Black American wife. Eventually, inevitably, he buckled.

As per the Tamil tradition, I was given his first name as my last name, but during their divorce, he requested that my mother change my last name to her maiden name. My mother was insulted that he would so blatantly deny his connection to me. She insisted that I keep the name, but she chopped it into a middle name and last name to make it easier for Americans who might struggle with a fourteen-letter surname. My father also gave me my first name, Sharada, after his mother—which was later modified by my mother to Sharda, after someone convinced her the extra 'a' in the spelling on my birth certificate must have been an error. This gave me the full name Sharda Chandra Sekaran.

I grew up embedded in the African American experience, enriched by the power of our culture and our profound history of suffering, struggle, and resilience. My mother, who never remarried, always had big ideas and aspirations for my future. I was close to my mother's parents. I loved my uncles and aunts, and my cousins became fill-ins for siblings. Still, I knew that some fundamental part of myself was missing.

The first time I met an Indian person was at an international cultural festival on Detroit's waterfront with my mother as a little girl.

Somewhere, there exists a photo of a tiny, shaggy-haired summertime me with a big smile on my face, posing next to a random woman in a sari.

When I was five, my mother and I moved to Queens, New York. Eventually, I found myself among South Asian classmates. Although I later made friends, I initially felt uncomfortable in their company and did my very best to avoid them. It was too much effort and too much agony to explain myself. I couldn't decide what I dreaded more—being the subject of their curiosity or being the subject of pity.

I remember when a girl named Deepa first approached me in junior high.

"You're Indian, aren't you?" she asked.

I flat-out denied it. I resorted to explaining my Indian name with nonsense about having hippie parents. I'm pretty sure she didn't believe me.

When I got to college, a woman from the Asian American mentor program showed up at my dorm room.

"We need more South Asian mentors," she said.

"I'm only half South Asian," I replied.

"Well, we need more mixed mentors too."

It felt a little random to me at first since I never considered myself to be Asian American, but I was curious. The mentor program connected me to a wonderful community and was a rewarding experience, but there was one moment that left me struggling. During a group training session, we were asked to create a family tree. I felt humiliated about participating with only half of my page filled out. I didn't even know the names of my father's family members. My knowledge stopped at the grandmother I was named after. That day, my heart was very heavy and I felt alone.

Since I helped my mother manage her bank records and saw the child support checks when he sent them, I knew where my father lived throughout the years. I never felt welcome to contact him, and he'd never tried to contact me. Our only communications were through court orders and paper trails.

I wrote to my father for the first time immediately after the experience I had in the Asian American mentor program in college. I demanded to know about his family tree, if only as my simple right to information about my lineage, no matter if he didn't have the guts to be in my life. I remember my letter being full of bravado and anger like he was my opponent in a rap battle, and I needed to flaunt my value and knock him down all at once. In my defense, I was eighteen years old, and I had reason to be angry.

I didn't expect a reply, but he wrote me back:

Received your letter and sorry for the delay. It was not easy. Wish you the best and I am very proud and happy for you. Below is the information you requested: My father's name is Sundaram Subraman and mother's name is Saradha Ramachandar. There is not any special name associated with them, and they are originally from the Southern part of India.

Take care.

Chandra

I felt like I was dissociating when I received the letter. It was there, typed on linen paper. His words. His signature. He was a real person. He gave me what I asked for, but it wasn't what I truly wanted. *What did I want? What did I expect?*

My estrangement from my father was a double burn because it was coupled with my estrangement from Indian culture and traditions. I felt a longing for a connection. South Asian food, philosophy, and arts pulled me like gravity. But like my first encounter with Deepa back in junior high, I was always uncertain about how to explain my background or engage with the community.

I've had a strong interest in travel and experiencing different cultures for as long as I can remember. My reward for going to the dentist as a child was a visit to the United Nations, which was across the street. As a teen, I begged my mother to let me attend a travel camp that filled the summer months with daily field trips around New York City and two long excursions to Canada and Florida. In high school, I took my first flight across the Atlantic on a student group trip. In college, I spent my junior year studying abroad in Paris and Zimbabwe. Much to my mother's distress, I took the rails across Europe and trekked through Madagascar and East Africa. I hiked a glacier in Iceland, lived with a family in Guatemala, and learned traditional dances from local children in a little Thai fishing village. I went anywhere but India.

During my senior year in college, I was a finalist for a travel fellowship, and my area of focus was the impact of Indian cinema on identity in the diaspora. I proposed going to Guyana, Mauritius, Fiji, and South Africa for research. I was curious to explore South Asian communities, but I felt like the only way I might find kinship was in places with people generations away from their origin.

During my interview with the selection panel, I sat at the end of a long oval table of academics who questioned me about my personal connection to the project and why I chose to exclude India from my proposed itinerary. I felt like my very identity was being put on trial. I didn't know how to explain the gaps in my story without bringing up my father's abandonment. I wasn't prepared to discuss that in front of a group of professors.

My skin burned with shame. I didn't want to start crying in front of them. I choked. I gave muddled and lazy-sounding answers.

"What happened? I thought I was throwing you softball questions," a South Asian professor asked me afterward.

I didn't get the fellowship.

～❧

I googled my father one day and found an article about him in his local newspaper. It was all about what a great dad he was. He was the head of the PTA, advisor of the chess club, and a chaperone on field trips at his daughters' school. The article portrayed him as a model parent.

I felt invisible and discarded. I found his email address. I contacted him again. I'm sure that I sounded like a bitter asshole in my email. Once again, I felt the need to preface my communication with a list of accomplishments, noting that they should all be credited to my mother with no help from him. He never wrote back.

Over the years, I would continue to google him here and there. Sometimes I'd do so during a moment when I was feeling particularly positive about myself. Other times, it was when I was feeling miserable and wanted to rub salt in my wounds. I also found his two daughters, my younger half-sisters, online. Eventually, I worked up the courage to contact them as well. Whether it was my defensive posture that turned them off or they were abiding by a family pledge of silence, they never responded to me either.

My final internet search for my father was seven years ago. It was roughly four years after that aborted flight from Atlanta to India. I found his obituary.

Apparently, he had only died a few months prior. I'm not sure how to describe how I felt upon uncovering this news. It was a strange combination of emptiness and regret.

I would have been reluctant to admit it, but I think subconsciously part of me secretly wished that my first trip to India would include a reunion with my father and his family. Perhaps I might finally even meet my sisters. But I felt like that dream died with him.

Regardless, I had to finally make this journey. No more excuses. I refused to let India continue to be a land that only embodied my father's absence. I made a plan to properly explore where half of my roots began.

I went to the airport, and this time, I made it onto the plane.

For a month, I traveled through Goa, Kerala, Tamil Nadu, and Karnataka, and I visited Mumbai for several days. The biggest shock for me was how at ease I felt. No one seemed primed to interrogate and shun me. Instead, I learned to become more comfortable with the proper pronunciation of my name, and each time I said it to an Indian, they seemed charmed and delighted to tell me about whichever Sharada they knew from their own lives or from the movies.

Although shopkeepers were occasionally flummoxed that I didn't know a single Indian language—"Really? Not even Hindi?"—they just assumed my lack of knowledge came from growing up in the diaspora.

I embraced the magic and the wildness and the bombardment of my senses. I fell in love with southern India, the beautiful brown and ebony glow of its people, and the land's hypnotic sunset colors. I was particularly smitten with Kerala and its wondrous tea-scaped mountains, blissful backwaters, and the palm-soaked shoreline presided over by massive birds of prey.

It was on this trip, on the very last day, that I bought a shimmery golden yellow sari and hoped that one day I would have a proper occasion to wear it.

Miraculously, after a series of frustrating attempts, my mother and I succeeded in draping that same sari around me on the morning of my wedding. It was beautiful, and it seemed symbolic that she and I could work together to honor the parts of my cultural heritage that felt both like missing and central aspects of my identity.

As we approached city hall, someone commented on my sari.

"What a lovely way to honor your father's culture," they said.

But, the way I saw it, I was honoring myself.

The following story contains sensitive material that may be triggering for trauma survivors. Domestic violence, abusive relationships, and PTSD are some of the topics mentioned in this author's moment.

If you feel triggered, please know there are resources to support you.

U.S. National Domestic Violence Hotline
1-800-799-7233

FOURTH AVENUE

BY HENA WADHWA

WHEN I WAS A CHILD, my father encouraged me to be a lioness, to be strong, fearless, and to stand on my own.

"Sherni bhun," he told me in Punjabi when I voiced my fears.

He would always reference the picture of the lion hung on the wall at home next to Durga Ma and Ganesh Ji. As my dad reiterated this phrase, I always thought of that picture. When I peeked at it, the lion appeared to look back at me, and at that moment I felt that it, too, had heard my dad's words and agreed.

Sherni. It came naturally at times. But my inner lioness was tested, especially on Fourth Avenue.

Fourth Avenue in Newark, New Jersey, was my street, my home, and my roots. Walking to the bodega, the beats of salsa, bachata, and merengue made me smile, and the smell of pollo guisado wafted from the storefronts. Everyone belonged, even the stray cats that made a home for themselves on the old, dilapidated wood porches.

My home was a safe zone with stability, Indian culture, and rigid rules. I would walk into my two-family house with barricades on the windows to the smells of masalas and my mom playing bhajans. However, Fourth Avenue had another face too. I learned about the harshness of life from the screams and cries in my community.

My neighbors were my first friends. Carmen and I met at two years old. Our childhood was full of the sounds of sirens, hip hop, and Spanish conversations between passersby. We drew hopscotch mats on the cracked and uneven sidewalks before running to the corner to catch the ice cream truck.

Carmen and I were close. But as we grew older, it became clear that I was different, and my mother never failed to remind me.

"You are Indian–remember this. You do not talk to boys. Focus on your studies," she'd say.

This response played in the back of my mind constantly. Between being a girl and an Indian, I felt angry. I felt alone.

"You must ask your father. If he says yes, then it's okay," was another line my mother would often use. It made me boil with anger as tears ran down my face.

"Why do I have to ask him? Why can't you give me permission?" I argued.

I envied Carmen's freedom and bitterly accepted that it would never be mine. As close as I was to Carmen and her family, my parents' cultural rules divided us.

What if I wasn't Indian? Would I get more freedom as a girl? The restrictions, the rules, and the control made me feel like a bird trapped in a cage.

At the age of thirteen, the rules changed again.

"You have to listen to what I say. I know what's best," my father would repeat in a stern tone.

"But I don't agree with you. Why do I have to do something I do not agree with?" I rebutted.

I began to question the gender norms in my house, and I could see his frustrated and disappointed stares. My younger self that lived for his approval and a "Shabash beta, I am proud of you" slowly left, and in her place entered a young woman who had questions and wanted answers.

"Why do we have to set up the plates? Why can't he? Why do men eat before us? I'm hungry," I would protest.

I stopped setting the table up and refused to pick up the dirty dishes. I was done. I looked at my mother and felt guilty. I witnessed her daily struggle of balancing her wifely duties with her career. I wanted to help, but I refused to act out a cultural script that left women forgotten and unseen.

When I went out, my struggles changed. Fourth Avenue looked different at fifteen than it had at five. There was a new wave of people moving into the neighborhood. I observed the harsh realities of poverty, domestic violence, sexual assault, forced abortions, and crime.

"What you looking at? We good?" a teenage boy yelled when I noticed him roughly handling his girlfriend.

It was understood that no one was to get involved. My Fourth Avenue—my home—had become a place of tears, sadness, unspoken violence, and grief.

One night, I was doing my English homework in my dad's den downstairs. As I wrote my essay, I heard a loud noise. At first, I ignored it. But then, I heard a woman screaming in despair. I ran to shut the lights off. Shaking, I peeked through the blinds.

I recognized him. He lived across the street next to my childhood babysitter. Tall, slim, muscular with full-sleeve tattoos.

"You want to piss me off, you want to do this," he yelled as he threw his fist up in the air, his large gold watch catching my eye. He repeatedly punched her face as she lay on the cracked concrete sidewalk, where her children had drawn a hopscotch mat, begging for mercy.

"Stop, please stop," she screamed. This fueled his anger as if she was wrong to cry and beg for her life. He grabbed her by her long, brown, curly hair that was usually styled so perfectly and dragged her down the sidewalk.

Why is he doing this? I thought. *Where is he taking her?*

Then, suddenly, I heard the loud cry of children. My eyes scrambled to find where it was coming from. And then I saw them. *How could I have not noticed them standing on the porch?*

They must have been only four or five years old. The girl held onto her dress as tears streamed down her face. The boy joined in and began to sob while their mother was beaten. A male family member held them back as they leaned to go toward their mother.

"Mami, mami," they yelled in unison.

"Hena. Breathe. Breathe, Hena," I whispered to myself. "Bhagwan, please stop this. Please have someone help her."

My chest tightened, and tears rolled down my face. I couldn't comprehend what was happening until her screams snapped me out of my daze. I looked over and saw her curled in a fetal position, trying to protect her head as he bashed it onto the concrete. He continued, unfazed, as her blood stained his clean white t-shirt.

She's going to die, I have to do something, she will die, I realized.

I ran over to the phone and hit 9, but I fell victim to the cardinal rule of Fourth Avenue—don't get involved. My finger trembled, and then I hung up. I cried, angry at myself. I held on to the phone, listening to the dial tone as I saw him drag her back into the brick house and slam the brown door. I knelt on the wooden floors of the den in the dark, rocking myself to calm down.

In school, I had learned that women's bodies were our own and that abuse is inexcusable. I heard the women of my family, of so many South Asian families, in that woman's screams and cries. Their stories of abuse, degradation, and violence were lived within me. I had failed all of them.

Fear took over my body, and I could not find my inner sherni. It was as if she did not exist. There were many times while washing the dishes I heard screams from my neighbor's house. In these moments, I ran to my room, cranked up my stereo system, and played the "Ruff Ryders Anthem." I fell into a daze listening to DMX's rap lyrics until the screams finally stopped. But this time, it was different. I saw everything.

My eyes and body witnessed a woman being beaten in front of her children. And I stood there and froze with the phone in my hand. *Why did I do that? What does that say about me?* I sat for what seemed like hours, crying and peeking through the blinds in case something else were to occur.

Maybe I can help then, I thought to myself.

I went to the bathroom and splashed cold water on my burning eyes. My chest tightened as I looked up to the mirror and could not make eye contact with my own reflection—I quickly looked down in embarrassment. There was no sherni. There was a fifteen-year-old girl who believed that the adversity of Fourth Avenue created an armor that prepared her to face anything. She was wrong. Sitting in the darkness, numb, tears wet my cheek as I retraced the numbers 911.

The next few days were a blur. In every direction I turned, I received a different message.

"It is our duty to educate women and your duty to support each other and every other woman," our dean said.

I felt myself cringe as if the universe was reminding me yet again that I had failed. *I did not support her. I tried, I wanted to, but I couldn't,* I thought. My guilt became an unwanted guest. *Why didn't you call, Hena?* I thought to myself as I replayed that night over and over. *What if he knew it was me? What would my parents say if I called 911? Would I get in trouble?* The questions never stopped.

My shame crept up every time I left the house as I avoided looking at or walking on that side of the street. I wanted to know if she was all right. I continued to peek through the blinds every night looking for her.

I wrote in my journal that I needed to do something, anything. My body froze as my mind recalled his punches hitting her body as she lay on the ground. I wanted it to stop—the thoughts, the flashbacks.

Shortly after, my teacher announced a new assignment—community service projects. We needed to volunteer at an organization in Newark every week. I began searching for neighborhood organizations and stumbled upon La Casa de Don Pedro.

On the website, I saw they were seeking volunteers for housing and domestic issues. While I wasn't quite sure what this meant, I wrote an email to the director indicating my interest. We spoke, and I was scheduled to meet with her after school.

"You should not be going over there," my father said. "The area is not the best. Stay home and focus on your studies."

I said nothing in return, just silently willed myself to follow through with my decision. *Go, Hena. Just go.*

The faded Burger King sign caught my eye as I got off the bus. La Casa de Don Pedro was right across the street. I walked into the center, indicated that I had a meeting with the director, and sat, wiping sweat off my palms as I waited.

What if my dad was right? Maybe this is a bad idea.

The director led me to her office and explained the center's new initiatives. They were seeking volunteers to assist with informational sessions for Hispanic and Latinx women looking to escape their abusers along with their children. With quivering hands, I signed the paperwork she gave me and agreed to begin in the summer. For the first time since the incident on Fourth Avenue, I felt at peace.

As I walked onto the bus returning home, I made a promise to myself that I would not ever let another woman down. I vowed to myself that no one, no man (including my father), woman, or societal expectation would dictate my journey, career, and identity.

As I walked along Fourth Ave, I saw the faded chalk drawings on the cracked concrete sidewalks. I glanced across the street, searching for the figure of the woman, praying as I did every day that I would see her and know that at least she was alive. She was nowhere to be found, but as I closed the metal black gates of my home, I felt a rediscovered part of myself emerge—my inner sherni.

The following story contains sensitive material that may be triggering for trauma survivors. Suicide is mentioned in this author's moment.

If you feel triggered, please know there are resources to support you.

U.S. National Suicide Hotline
1-800-273-8255

BORN UNTOUCHABLE

BY MEERA SOLANKI ESTRADA

WHEN I WAS INVITED TO SPEAK ABOUT IDENTITY AT AN INTERNATIONAL WOMEN'S DAY EVENT, I knew I wanted to include casteism in my talk. But, as I sat down to write my speech, I realized that I didn't know enough about my family's experience to begin. So I asked my dad to tell me more about his childhood, and it was only then that the stories started to flow.

"Beta, it wasn't that bad," he said, casually brushing me off at first.

But as I probed him further, he uncovered repressed memories, revealing more as his eyes filled with sadness. He spoke about my grandfather, with equal parts sorrow and pride.

"Your Bapa, Govind Solanki, was born in 1912—or maybe it was 1914," he said. "We're not quite sure, we didn't have any proper paperwork. But, never mind that. You see, because we were low, he couldn't go to school. Well, he could, but for people like us back then, we had to sit *outside* of the school and listen to the lesson. We couldn't go into the classroom."

I gave him a puzzled look, not quite registering.

"You see, beta, they thought untouchables were so dirty that even our shadow was impure. So even sitting outside the schoolhouse, if an upper caste person walked by, the Dalit kids had to lay face-down on the ground. That's what they thought of us. Dirt," he said, looking down.

"Dad, that's terrible."

"Beta, the world is cruel. Back then, so many children didn't go to school. Most kids just started working, like Bapa. Start poor and stay poor," he said with a shrug.

He told me how untouchables were forced into jobs that were considered unclean—from cleaning sewers and latrines by hand to clearing away dead animals. Such was the fate of my grandfather. Uneducated, he took up menial jobs for meager pay.

"Your Bapa worked hard, but he was sick with asthma. We didn't have money. He died. This is what happens."

I saw the sadness in my father's eyes as he recalled these memories.

"Asthma," I whispered to myself. A very treatable sickness, even in those early days, but for a poor, low-caste family, medication was an unaffordable luxury.

"Dad, can you tell me what it was like for you? Was it any better?" I asked.

"Oh, yes! I had some fun. I was a little mischievous, you know," my father said, a little upbeat.

He had told my brother and me some funny stories about his childhood antics, and I was hoping to lighten the mood.

"Tell me about school. I know you went to school...well, sometimes, at least," I said, with a sly smile.

"Ours was the era of segregation, so I could go *into* the classroom. But we had to sit on the floor in the back of the class. And when the master did the roll call, they didn't say our name, just BC for the backward class. That is the name we answered to. Even in all our schoolwork, we had to write BC after our name. They wanted to mark us."

I looked at my dad, mortified, feeling his shame and understanding for the first time why school may not have been the safest haven.

"Beta, at least it was easier for me than in Bapa's time." My father looked into the distance for a moment, then continued. "But sometimes we were so thirsty. It was so hot under that beating sun. The other kids could drink from the well, but we weren't allowed to. We had to ask the upper caste boys to pour water from high in the air into our mouths, while we kneeled underneath to catch a drink. They said our mouths were too filthy to touch the lota. Sometimes, we would run all the way home if they wouldn't give us water. Other times, we just waited until the end of the day. That was really terrible."

It was the first time I had heard my father express any resentment about his childhood.

"But we survived, beta." Always quick to slide out of a difficult conversation, he changed the topic. "Hey, why don't we talk about your mother? I was a very young man when we got married in 1976, only twenty-three years old. You know I'm a year younger than her, right?"

He loved to remind us of his youth in comparison to my mom.

"Your mother was studying her midwifery in England. We met when she came to India for a visit, and of course, she thought I was so handsome," he continued. "I looked good back then, you know, full head of hair. But your mother isn't lucky because of my good looks— she is the beautiful one. She's lucky because growing up in Kenya, she didn't go through the same abuse with caste as we did in India. Danji Bapa was a very smart man. He learned to read and write and moved his family out of India to Africa for a better life. Bapa was a very firm believer in education. You know this. Meera, that is the one thing to break the cycle of poverty. He wanted that for all of his children. And your mother and I worked so hard to have that for you two kids."

My mother had studied ferociously and eventually became a midwife, while my father furthered his education after marriage with another degree.

"We wanted to carve our own path and make our own identity, but sometimes these people don't want you to forget what you are born into—they want to keep you down, keep you low no matter what you do," my dad said.

There was a sadness in his face I had never seen before. I didn't want to probe more that day, so I asked if he had other memories he wanted to share and suggested he write them out for me. However, I got the feeling that this was enough of a trip down memory lane for him. I wasn't expecting that he would send me anything, but that same night, I got an email from him.

Attached was a six-page, hand-written letter detailing the experiences he wasn't able to share face-to-face. I cried when I read it.

There were two full pages dedicated to one particular incident:

When I was nine years old, I convinced my cousins to sneak out to the village prayers that were being held in an outdoor market. While Dalits were not allowed in temples or inside the homes of the upper caste, this was different—I found a loophole and wanted to be part of something special. We were so happy to hear the satsang and sat in the back, reveling in the excitement of finally attending a community event. But an upper society boy recognized us. He taunted our group, saying we were not welcome, and he loudly told us to leave. My older cousin was hot-headed and insisted that we be allowed to stay. But having a voice was not acceptable for us. An elderly man brought my cousin to the front of the large congregation and slapped him. It was supposed to be a public shaming and a lesson for all to see. We then ordered to leave. All they wanted was to humiliate us and make us feel like we were nothing.

❧

The shame of that incident changed the trajectory of my father's life, he revealed in the letter. He began to resent the treatment of his elders and insipid humiliation that he and his family and friends endured on a daily basis.

My father persevered, and in 1955, discrimination against untouchables was outlawed in India. He finished his primary school, then went on to high school, and eventually completed a degree in chemistry. He was the only person in his village at that time to go to university. He later went on to become a teacher at the same high school he attended. I felt the pain and pride emanating from these hand-written memories.

Reflecting on his letter, I couldn't help but remember when my parents told me and my brother about our hidden familial past.

When I was fifteen, my parents sat us down and said they had something very serious to tell us. With grave looks on their faces, they revealed our family lineage and explained that we were untouchables.

"Untouchable? What's that? I'm royalty," I hollered back, giving my brother a cheeky side-eye.

Up until that point, I would joke with my family that my obsession with fashion and prim and proper demeanor was because of my royal blood. We had read in history books about our ancestor, King Sidras Solanki, descendant of the mighty Chaulukya dynasty—all of which was true, but so was the royal's fall from grace, which I did not know about. Even back then, while my parents didn't share all the details of what they had endured as untouchables, they told us that we would have to work extra hard and be that much better because the world was not in our favor.

At that age, I had brushed it off as some antiquated notion, yet another outdated cultural belief that had nothing to do with me. But from that moment, something inside of me changed.

The chains of being an untouchable felt inescapable, even thousands of miles away in Canada. And the more I tried to distance myself from it, the more I noticed how people around me spoke about caste—sometimes in subtle ways, sometimes quite overtly. People even asked me which caste my family belonged to.

"I don't believe in that stuff," I would reply.

In some situations, the comments would praise my family's high status in society while degrading lower castes, not knowing that I was one of the very people they were insulting. And while I did my best to separate myself from all of its absurdity, it had become part of my identity.

I always questioned my worth in the back of my mind. I primarily dated Indian men, and with each new romantic prospect, I couldn't help but wonder what his family would think of me. *Was I too dark? More importantly, was I too untouchable?* I wasn't a fool. I'd seen the dating profiles seeking "fair-skinned, Brahmin girl." Looking back, I think I began to subconsciously gravitate toward non-Indians in my love life because I was fearful of being judged.

A few weeks after the email, I invited my father to the International Women's Day event. He was one of two men in a crowded room full of women. I had never intended caste to be such a big part of my speech, but it ended up becoming the anchor of it all. As I said the words out loud for the first time, looking across the room at my father, I saw how overcome with emotion he was. I wept for his wounds, and the entire room cried with me. Afterward, they gave him a standing ovation. Many people even went over and embraced him. I hugged him tight when I came back to my seat.

"Beta, I've never been so proud of you," he whispered.

That day we cried deeply, but we also healed in many ways.

While I have heard many privileged voices discredit the notion of caste or say that it holds no merit in our modern society, that is simply not the truth.

In 1989, the Indian government passed legislation known as The Prevention of Atrocities Act because discrimination against Dalits continued to remain so rampant. The act specifically made it illegal to parade Dalits naked through the streets, force them to eat feces, take away their land, foul their water, interfere with their right to vote, and burn down their homes. Yes, a law protecting against these specific acts of barbarity had to be passed because that was the reality of being born untouchable.

Today, one in six Indians is a Dalit, and they still experience such grave mistreatment that they are sometimes driven to suicide. Over the past decade, there have been twenty-two reported suicides by untouchable students from top universities. In 2016, a PhD student hung himself in his dorm room, leaving behind a note that read:

My birth is my fatal accident. I can never recover from my childhood loneliness.

We are still judged and labeled based on these assigned and unalterable social statuses—not just in India, but right here in North America. A couple of years ago, an acquaintance of mine in Toronto, who had recently used an Indian surrogate, told me while describing her experience with surrogacy that she would never choose low-caste women because she "wouldn't want to have a stupid child." I looked at her mortified, as I fought back tears. That conversation was a major turning point for me. I could no longer stay silent about who I was and the injustices that still exist.

I am not my circumstances. I alone define my identity. I refuse to let the caste system and bigotry of others weigh me down and inhibit my potential for greatness. Because, yes, I was born untouchable, but I am still a queen.

I'M HERE, AND I'M QUEER

BY NOVA A.

THE PERFECT BOYFRIEND

THE ECHOES OF HUNDREDS of sneakers squeaking and stomping filled the hallways after the school bell rang. I could already feel the sweat dripping down my neck. A scorching wave of heat burned my bare arms as I walked out of my air-conditioned middle school building. The sidewalk was littered with flower petals reminiscent of the marigolds scattered across the floor during Bengali weddings. I hurried to the bus stop where the trees offered some relief from the heat.

As I was about to turn the corner, I saw the dirty blonde beach waves belonging to one of the most popular girls in school. She was pretty, charming, and always smelled like Victoria's Secret body mist. I stealthily made my way behind her, then wrapped my arms around her waist, pulling her in for a hug. She squealed and giggled while turning to smile at me, revealing her perfect dimples. *Gosh, she's cute.*

I held her hand while listening to her attentively. She stopped talking abruptly, looked me up and down then said,

"If you were a boy, I'd kiss you. You'd be the perfect boyfriend."

I felt my spine straighten as the pride of having the most popular girl at school tell me she'd basically date me sunk in. I ignored how much that "if" stung and continued to act like the perfect boyfriend until we went our separate ways.

THE DECISION

I stared at my tweet for a few minutes.

`I'm coming out to my parents today`, it read.

My hand flopped down on the bed with my phone resting in my palm. I looked up at the ceiling, just breathing, waiting for the pressure on my chest to subside. It persisted. There was nothing special about that day, except that I had an impulse. I don't know what it was about that gloomy morning that beckoned me to come out. I had never found it necessary before. I always thought that they'd never have to know.

Navigating my identity as a LGBTQ+ individual within the desi community was not as straightforward as developing my identity as a Bengali-American. It was less exclamation points and more question marks.

Healthy discourse about sexuality is non-existent in my family. I was told to keep a distance from boys, and that was it. I just assumed

I was straight. *Muslim kids can't be queer,* I had always thought. Strict gender roles plague the Bengali community—if a young girl isn't soft-spoken or feminine, she is the subject of vicious gossip while boys who misbehave are "just being boys."

Living with a divorced single mother doesn't help the rumors either. That's what made adhering to those archaic gender specific rules seem so bizarre to me as a child. My mom put herself through school all while working, raising two daughters, and caring for her elderly parents, which is pretty badass.

My father is very nurturing and understanding, which is different from the toxic masculinity of the archetypal desi dad.

For the past few months, I had been frustrated after realizing that I was living in the double bind of the traditional desi community and heteronormative American society—both of which condemn queerness. I often felt like the token gay character among some of my friends who were straight, cis, and desi.

When voicing the possibility that I might be genderqueer, I found myself being dismissed or not being heard at all. It felt like a papercut, like I shouldn't be complaining about something so small, but it still stung.

I'm not even sure if some of my straight, cis, desi friends or acquaintances are allies to me, which is a little uncomfortable because I don't know what they really think of me sometimes. It's lonely to be the only queer person in the room when you're surrounded by people who look like you, but you still don't fit in and no one is making room for you.

❧

I have been out as bisexual to everyone but my family since I was sixteen years old, and I hardly gave much thought to sharing this information with my peers. But telling your parents something about you that you've hid for twenty-two years is nothing to be nonchalant about. Or, maybe it could be. I don't know, so I think of how the next few hours will play out: what I should say and how I should say it. The ringtone interrupts my thoughts. I pick up the phone.

"Assalamualaikum, Abu?"

THE SON

I decided I was going to wear a kurta for the first time. I thought back to a younger me standing in front of the mirror after pulling an oversized T-shirt over my head. I tucked my hair inside my grey beanie, pulling out a few pieces to frame my face. When I stepped back from the mirror, something didn't look right. My eyes traveled down to my chest. I frowned at the culprit of my body dysmorphia: the newly developed curves of my thirteen-year-old body. I pulled on one of my friend's old sweaters. The fabric hugged me in all the wrong places.

It'll be different this time, I told myself as I mentally prepared to accept how the kurta fit my body. I had begun to realize I am celebrated the most when I appear feminine or like a traditional desi girl. Somedays, I liked how that looked. Other days, it felt like I was wearing someone else's skin.

I was excited and nervous at the same time when I asked my father to help me buy my kurta. His face contorted in confusion, then irritation. My hope faded.

"That's not for girls. Why don't you want to get a regular dress?"

"They're all expensive and—" I said. Honestly, I couldn't think of any way to explain this to him. "I just want to wear one."

He didn't argue.

"It's fine. I always wanted a son anyway," he said.

Those sharp words pained me more than if he had just said no. I slowly sank into my seat as we drove off.

THE DECISION: COME GET ME

On the phone, my father's voice was gentle.

"Baba, tumi kemon acho? It seems like you aren't feeling good," he said.

"I'm not doing too good, Abu," I replied.

"What's wrong? Tell me."

I choked on words that never came out. It felt like my throat was full of sand. My father heard me whimper, and his voice started to waver.

"Abu, I don't know what I can do to make it better."

"Do you want me to come see you?"

I knew I needed his comfort, but I wondered whether his concern would turn to disgust if I confided in him. *Was it better to just suck it up and forget about coming out?* I knew that I couldn't go back once I did.

"Yes," I said. "Can you come get me?"

THE DENIAL

i like u too :)

I hit send as I grinned down at my phone, only looking up to make sure I'm not bumping into anyone on the stairs as I scurried to my next class. I had been texting this cute girl from a different middle school who had a crush on me. I feel like I could explode from the butterflies swarming my tummy. I need to tell someone. I spot my best friend, Maryum, in the halls and run to her.

"I've been talking to Gracie a lot. She said she likes me, and I like her too. I think I might be bisexual."

I was not expecting to be met with Maryum's scowl.

"You aren't bi," she said plainly.

The butterflies die. Instantly, I feel foolish. She walks away without another word, leaving me stunned, as I wondered why I even entertained the thought.

THE DECISION: NO GOING BACK

I stared down at my halal burrito bowl sitting in my lap during the quiet car ride to my father's home, wondering if I would be invalidated by him too.

He said he knew something was wrong when I had texted him—that when your child is feeling pain, you feel it, too. He didn't ask me what happened.

Once in the house, he set up the table for me to eat before disappearing into his room to take a call. My mind went blank, and my body was on autopilot as I shoved spoonfuls of rice into my mouth. *This could really change our relationship forever, but at this point, I can't say nothing,* I thought.

"Abu, I'm ready to talk," I said.

I lied. I wasn't.

"Bolo, ki hoise?" he said, as he sat down across from me. I paused.

"I don't want our relationship to change. I don't want you to be angry at me," I said.

"Whatever it is, I will try to understand," he said, looking at me reassuringly.

I took a deep breath. This was it.

"I like boys," I said, taking a deeper breath. "And girls."

THE POISON

"I am not marrying just any guy," I retorted. I grumpily sank into the couch, crossing my arms.

"Then what? Are you going to marry a girl?" my mom said playfully without taking her eyes off the natok.

I paused before I answered. I watched the Bengali couple on television bicker with each other. I was only in high school. Marriage shouldn't have even been a conversation yet. But, I realized it wouldn't be so bad. Women are considerate, beautiful, and smart.

"Well, if she's a nice girl that would be even better, no?"

My mother's head turned toward me so fast I thought it would snap off her neck.

"No! Never," she said with force.

"Well, what if she's pretty, smart, and is super loaded?" I asked sheepishly.

Her face hardened.

"Before you bring home a girl," she said in a dark tone, "bring me poison to swallow."

THE DECISION: CULTURE AND QUESTIONS

"Okay, I see," my dad said, adjusting his glasses. "You know, in our culture, this is not allowed."

"Yes, I know that, but it doesn't make me a bad person. This is just how I am."

"No, there are a lot of good gay people, but it is not really good. It is not permitted in Islam."

This was where I had anticipated the conversation going, but it wasn't as scary as I thought it was going to be. In fact, I was relieved. He didn't seem the least bit angry, disgusted, or close-minded. He was trying to understand. For the next hour and a half, we discussed misconceptions about bisexuality.

At one point, my father scratched his head and said:

"But if you like the girl, the boy will be mad. If you like the boy, the girl will be mad."

I tried not to laugh explaining to him that bisexuality isn't synonymous with polygamy. Coming out wasn't nearly as scary as I had anticipated. Half of it was trying to explain what my sexuality means.

Since that conversation, my relationship with my father has not changed. It feels like a privilege to have a progressive desi father who tries his best to be supportive. I still have not come out to my mother because she has been very clear she doesn't approve of homosexuality.

THE PARADE

I squeezed her hand while we ran toward the crowds waving rainbow flags and jumping to loud music that barely drowned out the cheers. That day, we were not a queer couple. We were just regular people in love. The streets were filled with color, glitter, and joy. The love in the air was palpable.

I had never felt anything like it, but I finally understood what I was missing in my life. It was this sense of unity and compassion among strangers, a safe space out in the open. We made our way to the front right, close enough to be able to mouth "I love you" to the parade floats and have air kisses blown at us. A woman rubbed bright magenta glitter on my cheeks, a drag queen made a heart with his hands at me as I blew him a kiss, and I hugged Ricky Thompson, an icon.

Euphoric tears filled my eyes, an unrestrained happiness burst in my chest and spread through me. We were all here because we deserved to unapologetically celebrate ourselves after being shamed into watering down who we are.

Let me introduce myself: "Hello, world. The name is Nova. My pronouns are they/them. I'm here, and I'm queer."

TERROR AND REDEMPTION IN TRUMP COUNTRY

BY J. LALWANI

"OH MY GOD! YOU'RE A TERRORIST," she screamed.

"I beg your pardon?" I asked, staring at her in disbelief.

"You look like a Muslim. You can't work for us. We believe in Jesus and America," my client said.

"Did you know Osama Bin Laden?" his wife chimed in.

"I don't. But I do know that you need to find another financial advisor," I said curtly.

I wish I could say being asked if I knew Osama bin Laden was an isolated incident. Or that I can count the amount of times I had been asked if I am a terrorist on one hand. I'm not what you would call a typical Indian. I am a divorcée who doesn't cook or believe in God.

Some might say I have become far too American, much to my family's chagrin. It was never my intent to be different. I just always found myself on the wrong side of what was expected.

My parents raised me to be a conventional Indian woman in the heart of Indiana. The constraints thrust upon my sisters and me were stifling. We were tasked with cooking, cleaning, and pretending to enjoy being silent. In hindsight, I was living a kind of spiritual suicide without knowing it. I grew up afraid of men, sex, and myself. I did not feel Indian. I felt more at home behaving as though I was not Indian. Not brown. Not different.

So, in 2016, when an unnaturally orange seventy-year-old man with a bad comb over and an even poorer disposition became the Republican nominee for president, I was horrified, but I still didn't believe he would win. His rhetoric was so divisive I could not imagine anyone agreeing with him, or at least admitting that they agreed with him. And it was with that naïveté that I started my new job in the heart of what I soon discovered was called Trump Country.

June in Phoenix, Arizona, is a scorcher. You can burn your hands just by buckling your seatbelt, left hot from the roasting desert sun, and the air conditioner never turns on fast enough. As I walked into my office, the air hung in my lungs like a gargoyle clinging to a gothic rooftop. I glided into the cool oasis of the lobby where two of my newest clients were waiting for me.

The wife was wearing beige capris and a white blouse. Gauche baubles of jade and yellow gold hung from her neck and ears. She was plain but carried herself with an unmistakable air of haughtiness. Her husband was dressed unremarkably but had a weathered leather Bible resting on his lap.

Unusual for a meeting with your stockbroker, I thought to myself, *but you get all kinds.*

I welcomed them into my conference room, and after a bit of small talk, we went over their portfolio. My assistant, Jane, round-faced and cheerful, brought their iced tea and shut the door.

"So, our previous financial advisor went to our church. Did you know that? Are you a believer?" the wife said. Her loud, staccato voice, similar to the plucking of a broken violin, echoed in the office.

"Did he? How nice for you. What church?" I replied.

"Do you believe?" she interjected.

"Believe? Believe in Jesus? Is that relevant?"

"Well, our church talks a lot about Muslims and how they are out to destroy Christians. Their Qur'an mandates they kill all Christians, so they can join Mohammed," she said matter-of-factly.

"Okay. Well, I'm here to help with your finances. If you don't think we are the right fit—"

"Will you read the Bible with us?" the husband interrupted.

"What? No," I said, aghast, standing up to usher them out the door.

The wife lunged at me and spat, her saliva splattering across my face and neck.

"Trump sees you for what you are. You're an evil terrorist who plots against us. But we will prevail. He will win. You need to go back to where you came from. God bless America!" she screamed.

"Jane, call the police," I said quickly to my assistant as I looked for a napkin and an exit.

I went to the bathroom, and my belly filled with shame. I listened to the banal chatter of other women while I stood alone, waiting for my turn to wipe the client's hate off my face.

Finally, I got to a stall and cried silently.

What was I crying about? I thought. Losing another client because of the color of my skin? No. Not that. Not really. Was I crying because she spat on me? Partly.

There was something else though. Something far more upsetting. My makeup was smeared, and I splashed my face with cold water, hoping I could wash this feeling off me. As I wiped my face clean and looked in the mirror, I saw someone I didn't recognize looking back at me. She was Indian. Brown skinned. Dark eyes. It was *me.*

But I didn't know *her.*

The police came. The female cop was ginger-haired, and the male policeman spoke with a slight lisp.

"What seems to be the problem, ma'am?" the female officer asked.

"She is a terrorist," the wife said.

"I absolutely am not a terrorist!" I snapped back, my face still damp from washing it, now reddened.

"What proof do you have, ma'am?" the male cop said with a lilt looking at the wife.

"Well, look at her! That's what they look like," she screamed.

The officers seemed more sympathetic to the wife's cause than mine. They asked for my license and spent a great deal of time querying my upbringing and how long I had lived in the United States.

In the end, they did not arrest me.

The woman got a warning, and the officers told me "to be aware of who I am speaking to."

I felt numb when I finally got home. I couldn't cry or watch TV. I just stared at the walls and could hardly believe what had just happened. Realizing that I needed to work the next day, I took an extra dose of cough syrup and drifted off.

The shame lingered, though, and settled into bitterness as the weeks passed and more clients fired me for being Indian.

"Can we trust someone like you?" another potential client asked me.

Even before things hit a crescendo with my latest client and her spittle, others had refused to sit with me when they saw my foreign name.

I felt like I was completely alone and unwanted. Every time I looked at my reflection, I questioned the person I saw. *Had I always been this dark? Who was this person staring back at me?*

I don't believe in ghosts, astrology, or any other form of hocus pocus tomfoolery. And yet, my face was changing, dramatically, sometimes by the hour. How does a person explain to the world her face is morphing into that of a stranger?

I was losing the best parts of myself to some force I could not stop, and the world kept moving. I became increasingly withdrawn, and even when my friends would reach out, I didn't respond.

But, one of my friends didn't take the hint too well to leave me alone, instead opting to storm into my office to confront me for not returning her many calls. She was my very wise, very honest, and very white friend.

"What the hell, Julie? What's going on with you?"

"You are the last person I want to talk to right now," I shrugged.

"Why? Because I call you on your bullshit?"

My temperature started to rise.

"My bullshit? You wouldn't know bullshit if it smacked your ass."

"Try me! If you have something to say, say it. If you're mad at me, have the courage to tell me why," she demanded.

"Courage? What the fuck do you know about courage? You spent your life enjoying the privilege of being a white woman. You have been taught that your feelings, goals, and body matter. You are treated as the standard for beauty around the world. No matter how unattractive a white woman is, she is still considered more beautiful than most women of color. You have been raised to think if you want something, it is your right to go for it. You have been nurtured to believe that it is your birthright to run the world. You have the privilege of treating racism like it's an academic problem.

"Your sense of entitlement extends so deeply that you think you are owed an explanation for me not wanting to speak to you. Who the fuck are you to demand anything from me? How are you better than me? More beautiful than me? More worthy than me?

"Get out. Get out of my office. Get out of my life. I am not your pet to trot out to make your liberal sensibilities feel better. And as the door is shutting on your ass, I want you to remember that the courage of one thousand white women could not touch the strength and determination of one woman of color. But unlike you, we don't expect anyone to care."

All the color drained from my friend's face as I screamed at her. She had always been a lighthouse to me in times of difficulty. We had bonded as women who wanted more from life and ourselves.

I collapsed to the floor and started crying. It felt like this rush of emotion had been lifetimes in the making. All I could do was weep for all the time I had wasted thinking I was less than because I am an Indian woman. For a moment, it felt like all that existed was this—my friend and I in my office, tucked away from the noise of the rest of the world.

"You're right. I have been given a lot at your expense. I am so very sorry for how you've been treated. And for what it's worth, I've always thought you were beautiful," she cried, holding my hand.

If you can imagine a large glass window shattering into hundreds of shards, that's what her words felt like in my heart. For the first time in months, I felt less alone. I could breathe. It wasn't my friend's apology that mattered, it was her giving me the space to be angry at her for how racism had wreaked havoc in my life. She met my anger with compassion and kindness. She stood with me as I implicated her, her family, and her history in the experiences that led to my deep abandonment of my Indianness.

Later that night, after consuming copious amounts of cheese and chocolate wafers, I looked in the mirror. I recognized bits of my face for the first time in months.

Racial bias has been a kind of horror-ridden enchantment that has kept me from living, loving, and exploring who I am. The greatest prejudice I have ever experienced was the voice in my head that bellowed at me that I am not good enough as I am. That I needed to bleach my skin or feign interest in things like barbecuing, ugly sweater holidays, or *Real Housewives of God-knows-where*.

And, oddly, it was a white woman's kindness that broke the spell for me. She did not give me my identity. No one can do that. But her compassion gave me the space to start to reclaim it. The first step in my journey back to myself was anger. Anger at the injustice of racism. Anger at the world that perpetrated its lies. Anger at myself for the time I have wasted in believing it. I choose to no longer be cornered or marginalized.

It was then I realized that not only does racism exist, but it hurts the most when you believe it. Racism thrives when you internalize it—what is wrong today was hate yesterday and will be a tragedy tomorrow. It triumphs when you experience it and choose not to fight for your life or those like you. I choose to fight.

COMING TO
AH-MERRI-KAH

BY AMRISA NIRANJAN

DO YOU REMEMBER WHEN YOU MET YOUR MOTHER?

I do.

It is 1993. The air is hot. Not normal hot—it is hot-hot. In Guyana, that is how we explain when something is even more—you say it twice, even three times if you have to. No need for extra words when saying the same one works just as well. Grandma uses more words though. But I don't have as many, and I don't need them anyway.

I am four, nearly five. I was born in October. I have not met my mother. These are the facts I know. Well, I know I did meet her, but, you see, I was a baby, and that does not count, because nothing counts when you are a baby. You are just a brown little person; you might be light brown, like maybe your mother is raw cane sugar, or even darker brown, like maybe cassareep was your father, but you are just a baby, and nothing you do really counts, even when you are bad. And babies can be very bad sometimes. But they don't get in trouble. So maybe I did meet "your mommy" like everyone calls her, but it didn't count because I was a baby. Maybe she counted it. I don't know. I don't know much about her.

Grandma and Aunty Shenny tell me to say "I love you" to her and my dad on the phone sometimes. There is a staticy silver noise sound when I take the phone. Mommy says nice things, and her voice is good, not good like Grandma's—whose voice is sweet with a pitch that sounds like if molasses could sing. But Mommy's voice is good, and I know she is real.

"I love you," I repeat on the phone.

I don't know about love really, though, except I know I do love my dolly. She is a white baby. I have never seen a white baby, but I don't care. She could be a cane sugar or Marmite skin baby—she is my baby. I love her little pink stroller, and I love walking her round and round the house like I am her mommy. We have important things to do. And my dolly came from my mom and dad, so I suppose I could love them, too.

Dolly came like all my special things came. In a big brown barrel. Every now and then a tall tan paper barrel comes. Uncle Romesh comes over, and other people too, and it's something like an unscheduled Christmas. It comes any time of year, but it feels the way your birthday feels. And you even have to take pictures, too. They are to show Mommy and Daddy.

We get a surprise of presents inside the barrel. Some presents are stupid, like ketchup and macaroni and cheese boxes. But Grandma likes them. She seems smart to me, so I don't know why she likes these bad presents, but she does. I get lunchboxes and sneakers for presents too. These are not as bad as ketchup, but not as good as a dolly.

Some presents are not for me, some are for my sister, Ari. I don't know why but I get jealous. I can play with her barrel presents—she isn't mean and she shares, but I am jealous anyway. Maybe because

Ari got to meet Mommy and Daddy already, so why does she even need more presents?

So, Mommy and Daddy, they live in Ah-merri-kah. It is far. Even though I never met them, I do know how they look. They are in a frame by the big blue chair. Everyone special has a picture in the house. But their picture looks fancy. I don't know how I know, but I think it's because they are dressed up. He is in a suit, and she has a dress on in the picture, and they are in a fake outside. It doesn't look like any outside I see, but it's probably how outside looks in Ah-merri-kah.

Mommy is pretty. She has red lipstick. I don't wear lipstick, except when Aunty Shenny puts it on me to play dress up. But Grandma wears hers almost every day. It is red, but not like the hibiscus flower red—it has something else in it, something that makes it look more like a nighttime red. I like watching Grandma put the shiny crayon to her lips and trace her mouth while looking in the mirror. It is something special to see, because most of the time she is home and she has on old shirts dirty from working outside and big shorts she wears when she is looking after her cherry tree and her roses. I look after the sunflowers, but never mind that now. When Grandma is ready, though, she transforms herself into a red lipstick angel and she wears pretty, pressed shirts with her grown-up lady skirts. So Mommy must do it, too—transform herself with her lipstick. But I haven't seen her do it yet, so I don't know for sure. I just suspect.

Daddy, he is in the picture too, but he is not pretty. He is just a man, and I don't know if he is handsome, but he is not ugly. He has a mustache. It is black, and his hair is black. He is smiling. They both have perfect teeth, but you cannot see Daddy's as much. His skin and her skin are brown like cane sugar, but I am a little darker, and so is Ari. We are all different browns, and that's why my dolly can be white. Just because your mommy is one color doesn't mean you will be the same one.

It is August. It is still hot. But I am wondering when it will rain. I am hoping soon because I want our metal and plastic barrels to fill up with water. The brown barrels are good for playing in. You can go inside and make someone else roll the barrel while you tumble around and around. You think you might get hurt, or maybe just Grandma thinks you will, but you never do.

They are not good for catching water, the brown barrels. But we are like barrel keepers, and we have many of them. When the blue plastic one outside is full from rainwater, you can jump in it. I can't go in alone because I'm not tall enough, but Ari and Uncle Teddy can hold me up inside, and it is not scary like swimming in the canal. It is cool, and I can wiggle my feet in the water and imagine I am a mermaid.

When it rains, you don't have to wait for the barrel to fill—you can take off all your clothes and you go outside naked in the yard and run all around. And the mud comes squishing up between your toes, and the thick grass blades are softer, and all the hot ants are hiding and can't even bite you even though you're naked skin. No one seems to be thinking about the rain, though. Everyone seems busy.

Grandma tells me we are going into town to buy me an outfit for the plane ride to Ah-merri-kah. I knew one day I would go because everyone always tells me I will go and meet my mommy and daddy someday, but when grown-ups tell you words like "someday" and "one day," you never know when they mean and even they don't know. That's why they say it like that. It isn't a lie, though.

Grandma drives us into Georgetown. We go up the bumpy, bumpy road. Sometimes the car goes up and sometimes it goes down, and then we are on the smooth road going to the busy marketplace with all the stalls and the place where the cows are hanging from big hooks with all their skin taken off. I hate to look at it because it is so scary, but I get so excited to see it every time, and that is a weird feeling to want to see something you don't really like to look at.

Today isn't for meat though. Today is for clothes for me and Ari, too. The "someday" and "one day" is soon. I know it's coming because Grandma is running into town all the time, and we have to go to one hundred places to get one hundred things. Grandma has to talk to everyone for nearly one hour and I have to wait, so sometimes it's boring and I don't want to go to town, but today, I don't mind because I get to help pick my outfit for the plane. We always have to buy the same thing for me and Ari but in different colors. It is good one of us isn't a boy or we would look schupidy—that's a better way for saying stupid. I already think we look a little schupidy in the same clothes, but I also like being the same as Ari. She is smart because she's bigger than me but not so big like a grown-up. She also has been to Am-merri-kah, so she knows what we should wear. I pick a black and yellow skirt and shirt set with flowers. Ari gets the same thing, but hers is red.

Then the "someday" comes. I am sad. You see, when someone goes to Ah-merri-kah, we have a party at the airport. It is like when you go to the creek—a dark rum-colored river with sandbanks to play on—and you go with all your coolers and your cook-up rice. Except you do it with all your best friends and family right in the parking lot by the airport. You even play music from one of the minibusses. A minibus is how you get around town, and if you know someone who drives one, they will help you come to the airport with all your suitcases.

I am sad, though, because something feels sad, even though I'm happy to go meet my mommy and daddy. Maybe it is because Uncle Ted and Aunty Shenny also seem a little bit sad. *When will I see them after this?* I am starting to wonder if my new "someday" will be when I will see *them* again. When will I see my favorite cousins, Lisa and Tracy, again? My ajee? They are not coming to Ah-merri-kah with me today.

❧

Then we go on the plane. Me, Ari, and Grandma. It is okay if I go anywhere, as long as Ari comes too. We get to the biggest, whitest, cleanest place I have ever seen in my whole life. It is JFK airport in New York. It is still August, but it is not hot-hot here.

Then, I see *her*. She is in a white suit but with a skirt. She is just like the picture, and she has lipstick. Daddy has on a yellow and black shirt and black pants. They are so perfect—they are just like their picture. I am sitting on the suitcases, and Mommy has even brought me a small balloon.

"Are you my real-real mommy?" I ask her.

"Yes, I'm your real-real mommy."

Twice. She said it twice.

Daddy doesn't say much. I don't say much to him either.

Ari is here. Grandma is here. Mommy and Daddy are real.

I am tired, but I have to see everything. Ah-merri-kah is lights at night—bright little dots, some red, yellow, some like blue. We did not have so many, even in Georgetown, my first real city. We drive for a long-long time. The moon chases us as we go, just like it did in Guyana, behind the clouds, then peeking out again. So some things are still the same, no matter where you are. We drive, and the car does not even bump up and down like in Guyana. Everything in Ah-merri-kah is better—this is why we came. For smooth road rides and bright lights at night that always stay on.

❧

Mommy and Daddy don't sound like Grandma. They sound like the white people on TV, like what dolly would sound like if she got big and could talk. They live in an "uh-part-ment"—it is a small-small house. They are videoing me and Ari, like we are movie stars.

"Is it recording?" Mommy says. *Recording? She must mean videoing.*

There are a lot of new words here, and they mix them in with the ones I know already. Ari knows more of the words than me. I sleep at night and dream of Guyanese fruit stands by the roads with holes. I even dream of the dust coming up as the cars go by.

Days and days and days go by. I think I have enough words, but Ari knows I don't. She makes me mad because she is making me learn new words, and I have enough words. This is stchupidy or "stoo-pid"—there are always two or even three words for one thing in Ah-merri-kah. Extra sounds for nothing at all, except to make you mad and waste your time.

But Mommy and Daddy only use the Ah-merri-kah words when they talk to me and Ari. And I want to sound like them. I don't even know if they like me. And I feel bad because I'm sure they must, but I feel shy to talk to them at all, like when Grandma pushes you to say hello to a grown-up you do not know. But I try to learn because I want them to like me, even if I do not know them.

What's the word for a molly, the style of hair that I wanted—u circle twist of hair tied at the top of my head—I think. What do they call it here? A plait is a braid. What is a molly called in America? Ari teaches me the correct word is bun—like when you bun yourself on the fireside.

I don't know if to laugh or cry, thinking that some words have changed altogether. A Guyana bun is a burn. A bun is a molly. I think to myself, sometimes—but only while looking at my toes, because I don't want Mommy, Daddy, or even Ari to know or see it in my eyes—that I *don't like it here always.*

My old words are a secret. And in a place with so many lights—lights that always stay on—you cannot use your dusty old words. I need more words, new words, shiny and big, like JFK Airport. When you want to keep something secret, you bury it in the yard. I did this too, but in the yard inside my head. I don't like Ah-merri-kah always, but I want to stay. I want to stay where Ari is, and with Mommy who is pretty, and Daddy who is quiet.

So I forgot the first words Grandma taught me. And I learn that you don't say things twice to mean them more. You find a newer, fancier word instead. It's not good-good, it's great. It's not bad-bad, it's worse. Sometimes I forget to forget. Mommy and Daddy do too. They speak like Guyana, but not to me. Never to me. Only to aunty this and uncle that, or whoever else is from Guyana. It's like a game, maybe. A forgetting game. And the more you forget, the more you win. The more fancy words you know, the more sure you can stay in Ah-merri-kah.

But I don't always remember to forget. The dentist—he's a doctor for your teeth—asks what I ate one day.

"Dhal and rice and bhajee," I say proudly, loud and clear.

Ari looks like she might just fall over. She wants me to say lentils, rice, and spinach—or maybe not even that—but she didn't teach me those words yet. The dentist is confused, but he smiles. His teeth are big and white, not like mine. I have some brown teeth from Guyana, and that's why we came. Teeth give away your secrets too.

Did you know that in Ah-merri-kah, even your whole name changes? I am now "Am-reese-uh" or "Am-riss-uh" or

"Ah-mar-iss-uh." I decide I'm "Am-riss-uh" because it is cleaner than the "Ahm-reese-uh" sound—the one that gives away my secret, the way my name was said in Guyana. Even Ah-merri-kah does not keep its name. It is "Uh-mer-ih-cuh"—so everything gets new names here. But who cares. There are so many channels. Everything you trade, you get something back in Ah-merri-kah, and there is a lot to trade.

Your secret isn't just hiding in your sound. It hides in your clothes too. My suitcase had my warm sun clothes, some Mommy and Daddy had even sent me. But maybe too much dust from Guyana came with me, because even my clothes are not allowed here. We go to the mall— it is the word for an inside market where the stalls are all so big you can go inside. Imagine your whole family and you inside one shop. And it is not made of wood. Not much here is. And we go to the GAP, and we buy bright one-color things, boring things, things to make us more like a "Katie" and less like an "Amrisa"—so it is good. I already gave up my name, what is a little bit of clothes?

I win the forgetting game. I learn each day which new part to trade— today two words, tomorrow just the way you say a single letter might do. And I don't care. I am now near six, and I can trade teeth, shoes, and even Grandma. I can give away hammock swings, because now I get playgrounds. I can trade whole months of sun. I can give anything.

My presents come from stores, not barrels, and all my lights can go on at any time I want because now I am in Ah-merri-kah, and I am here to stay. I give away my old words, and I can give them away even faster than Ari can.

I win. I win. I am even beating her at forgetting. I never say my middle name. And I will trade more and more and anything, anything, everything, everything, and I know, I know, I will do it again, and again, because now I get Mommy and Daddy and Ari, and I get Ah-merri-kah too.

HARRISON ROAD

BY RADHIKA PATEL

"HA! WE WON, WE WON. NO MORE IMMIGRANTS," my aunt said, sounding as though she had beat me in a child's playground game.

A mug of tea in hand and eyes burning, I tilted my head away from the beam of sunlight, which shot through the kitchen window. I was shaking with anger and confusion. My hands were barely keeping the phone pinned against my ear. My lips felt warm, emotions readied and waiting to burst out of them at any given moment. *Don't say anything stupid. She's your masi.* I hung up.

I drew a deep, stomach-expanding breath. One of those inhalations that physically consumes you, that seeps into the nooks and crannies of your tired body, resting momentarily in spaces that you didn't even know air could reach.

And as blood pumped into my ears and head with a rhythmic desperation for release, it carried her tune, repeating it over and over like a dull thump to the brain.

"No-more-immi-grants."

On this day, more than half the U.K. decided to withdraw from the European Union, a day marked by a racist campaign against immigrants, reminding swathes of the population and my masi of the good old days, of imperialism, of life without us, of life as the real Britain. A real Britain, without my masi. This day came fast and through the wires of a telephone line one hundred miles away.

"No-more-immi-grants."

At least there are 48 percent of us grimacing at our tepid tea, I thought. A futile sense of solidarity passed over me as I emptied the mug into the sink. *Not masi though.* Bitter and salty tears flowed, coating the basin in a glossy sheen, draining away with the sweet tea and our family's history.

My masi's voice still reveled, playfully in rolling R's, mockable mispronunciation, lilted sentences, and hybrid languages picked up along the way. My masi's bony, feeble-looking frame and sallow cheeks were an illusion, encasing an interior strong in nerve and spirit. My masi bounced around her house, offering boxes of kadju katri, fafda, and cups of chai that could heal you with every sting to the throat from the spicy masala.

"No-more-immi-grants."

In a defiant decision to leave behind that turbulent and confused churning in my head, I walked up the stairs to my bedroom. I perched myself precariously on the edge of my bed, looking for any object that might provide a momentary escape from my thoughts. *Music's too intense,* I decided, staring at a pile of CDs on my desk. *TV?* I pondered, eyeing my laptop. *But what would I even watch?* I glanced at my bookshelf.

Boxy books of distraction sat cushioned on the shelf ready for the taking. *Harry Potter.* I got off my bed, strangely excited and stretched up to retrieve the final installment from its dust-settled spot. I opened it in the middle. As sunlight poured in through the window, I could feel my limbs slowly loosen with every turn of the page.

It was in these same stories that I had found comfort in, a decade ago, from the chaos of bustling bodies at the house on Harrison Road, one hundred miles away in Leicester. And as I turned another page, I was transported back to this familial home, where my masi still lives.

It was located in the heart of the Gujarati immigrant community from East Africa, fondly dubbed Leicester's Little India. The house on Harrison Road had washed-out rangoli etched onto its concrete steps outside and a cast of characters that drifted in and out of it over the years.

As a child, I ran my hands across its bumpy, textured wallpaper, pressing down with the tips of my bitten nails, surreptitiously marking my territory on the reliefs of this monumental site of stories and events. I memorized the shapes of the floral wallpaper, the twisting petals and contorted leaves that crossed each other with menace and beauty. I fought with my cousins and made up with them over a game of seven stones with shiny marbles that looked like the sweets bapuji would buy us secretly. I ate my fill while my brother was scolded for taking too long to finish. I watched as the women flicked out atta from under their haldi-stained nails and the whole family gossiped about last week's wedding.

And then sometimes, I would lock myself away from it all in my masi's bedroom so I could read.

"Leave her, let her read," my mum said in muffled tones from beneath the laminated floors of masi's bedroom. There was a warm smell of rotli and butter that drifted like a thick fog through the floor, as well as the usual din of the kitchen—clanging pots and pans, a ruckus of laughter, and loud conversation in English, Gujarati, and Swahili. Her bedroom would become my sanctuary for hours.

In this house, in this bedroom, my masi shared her stories about her travels, of the food and customs of those around the globe. She would tell me that, one day, she would take me with her because "no one else appreciates history in our family, Radhu." Her eyes would recede to her forehead as she scoffed in annoyance at my mum, uncles, cousins, or anyone showing the smallest sign of boredom or frustration at the fiftieth photo of a Thai temple. I would laugh along with those mocking her but secretly always enjoyed the youthful passion and color that it brought to her face, which had faded with age.

She'd once found an old cardboard box of photos buried deep in a cupboard above her bed. We sat together with my mum trawling through them. They sighed, smiled, and laughed as they relived their childhood memories.

"Where's this photo from?" my mum said.

"Can you guess who this is?" my masi asked.

Her life and my family's lives were ingrained in every inch of each photo and in every object within the walls of the house on Harrison Road.

But in that house, in that room, I also listened to stories aching with sadness, a collective trauma masked by tough skin. I heard the story of how mama was blinded in one eye by a group of knuckle dusters and skinheads, and I learned what the term Paki-bashing meant. They recalled what it was like to have shit thrown at their house and be denied entry into places because of their skin color. These stories, seared into my brain, taught me about the realities of being an immigrant.

My family was forced to leave India after Britain chewed up and spat out their homeland. After finding a new home in Uganda, they were cast out and expelled. Then they fought to stay in the U.K., a country that didn't want them—where they brought up children and took punches so their kids wouldn't have to. But now, they were British once and for all.

I rolled over, lifted my body from my bed, and closed the book.

It repeated a final time in my head now—slower, less muddled, but spiked with more pain than I had ever considered existed in those three words.

"No more immigrants."

These were the words of a woman persuaded that she was never one. With the snap of a finger, just like that, with one vote, a woman's history was erased. Her family's history was erased. My history was erased.

As the walls of Harrison Road broke down in my mind, I took another deep breath, got up, and started to get ready for work.

AN "AMERICAN"

BY SHIMUL CHOWDHURY

ON A BRISK FALL MORNING IN THIRD GRADE, I showed up to school in my mustard-yellow lehenga instead of the mandatory uniform—a plaid skirt and collared top. I walked through the halls with shaky knees and headed for the school media center instead of my usual classroom. As I passed students sitting in the hallway, I heard muffled, yet distinct whispers about my outfit choice:

"Doesn't she know Halloween's over?"

Accustomed to this kind of treatment, I brushed off their words and didn't bother to stop and explain myself. A group of teachers were waiting for me in the media center and ushered me into the back studio area dedicated to the production of the morning news segment. There, I found a line of other students of color, all dressed in cultural garb and looking as confused as I was.

The morning news at my elementary school in South Florida was a full production with professional cameras, backdrops, and even teleprompters. On a typical day, student anchors relayed club activities, lunch menus, and quirky inspirational quotes. The resulting show was viewed in every classroom at the beginning of the day—but today's show was different.

The week before, a teacher asked us to come to school wearing "ethnic clothing" and said we had been handpicked for a special broadcast. Despite the mystery surrounding the segment, a part of me was thrilled. This was my chance to show off my best outfit to my peers, and I was flattered by the idea of being recognized in front of my whole school.

Grasping the fabric of my lehenga, I waited for the teacher's direction on what I should do next.

"Walk to that X marked on the ground, look at the camera, and read off the teleprompter," she told us.

One by one, the other students stepped under the light and read off the screen. When it was finally my turn, I walked forward, carefully making sure I didn't trip over the length of my skirt. I stared into the camera lens and recited the words scrolling in front of me:

"My name is Shimul, and I am an American."

I felt breathless, exhilarated, and a bit embarrassed. The program continued as more students stood on the mark, proclaimed their nationality, and rushed back out of the frame. I am certain that a teacher closed the segment by delivering coded remarks about 9/11, patriotism, and community.

Perhaps they said, "America is a melting pot and we should all stick together."

Or something laughably reductive like, "We are all the same."

Looking back now, I see what I could not have possibly known as a child—that on that day in November 2001, my school, my teachers, and my community had all failed me.

❧

My memories of the months after 9/11 are scattered. I remember my mother, who had never listened to the radio in the car, cranking the dial when she picked me up from school. We learned the details of the tragedy that day from a breaking news report that blared through the speakers—we were stunned into silence. Every morning after that, both of my parents attached American flag pins to their clothes before they went to work at the gas station they managed. They would hastily pin a red, white, and blue ribbon to my shirt as well.

I remember talking to my older brother at school and being interrupted by kids shouting,

"Go back to your country, Osama!"

I remember the rustle of my lehenga when I sat uncomfortably in class after the morning news aired, aware of the stares and whispers around me.

After 9/11, South Asian kids who *looked Muslim* to the general population were tasked with convincing everyone we knew that they were safe around us, that we were not one of *them*, that we belonged in the United States. If we stuck patriotic ribbons onto our clothes, maybe we would receive one less scathing glance. If we watched the news that condemned us every night, maybe we could better understand our nation's hatred.

For most of the past eighteen years, my strongest memories of post-9/11 Islamophobia revolved around overtly negative encounters—punching a classmate in the face when he called me a terrorist in the seventh grade, neighbors screaming at my Bangladeshi mother to go back to Afghanistan, constantly having to respond to inane questions and comments.

"How do you feel about Sharia law?" people would ask me. "Tell me about jihad."

But on that autumn day at school, I was asked to proclaim my sameness in front of the entire student body—and therefore, I was put into this unmistakable position of defense. I was forced to assert that my U.S. American identity, previously unshaken and unquestioned, was legitimate. I was made to arrive in costume, dressed up to highlight my otherness.

This otherness came with new responsibilities. I now seemed to represent not only a global religion but also all the negative attributes of my ancestral homeland—even though I was born in the United States. Along with the already burdensome role in which I was unexpectedly cast, I also had to contend with well-meaning but misinformed adults, like the very teachers who turned my identity into a spectacle, forever marking me as the Muslim girl.

Though I had experienced being marginalized by my peers before that segment, I still felt like I was connected to my school and community. But that November morning, I lost my sense of belonging. And why? Because my yellow lehenga, black curls, and unusual name were too different? Too threatening?

Sometimes I replay that day in my head and wonder what it would have been like if things had been different. It would go like this:

On a brisk fall morning in third grade, I showed up to school in my usual uniform. I was especially excited that day because I had been handpicked for a special broadcast along with a few of my classmates. I walked through the halls and headed for the school media center, joined by the others who would be taking part. As I passed students sitting in the hallway, I heard muffled, excited whispers about the newly released *Harry Potter* movie.

"I just saw it yesterday! It was so good."

"Don't ruin it."

A group of teachers waited for me in the media center and ushered me into the back studio area dedicated to the production of the morning news segment. There, I found a line of students of all races, discussing the usual third-grade issues—lunch money, playdates, the complexities of learning to write in cursive.

We were directed to all stand on a giant X marked on the ground, wait for the signal, and then read off the teleprompter in unison.

We all lined up in rows so we could fit into the camera's frame. Some of us stood, others kneeled, and I sat firmly on the ground directly in the center.

The teacher gave us a thumbs-up, and we all shouted:

"Welcome to the morning broadcast, here's the latest news."

UNVEILING ME

BY GABRIELLE DEONATH

I'VE BEEN THINKING ABOUT doing something drastic, and I don't know who else to talk to about it.

Sitting on my bed, I signed the email and pressed send.

Even though it was 9 p.m. on a school night, my high school guidance counselor responded almost immediately:

Gabbie, please stop by my office first thing in the morning.

The next day, I walked into the big brick school building, and as the bell for first period rang, I made my way up the steps to the administration floor. Halfway down the long hall, I opened the door to my left and greeted the receptionist.

"Hi dear. How can I help you?" she said, smiling.

"Ms. Gottfried asked me to see her. I didn't have time to sign up for an appointment," I replied.

"She's been expecting you. You can go right in."

The student body of my high school in Long Island, New York, was 49 percent white, 49 percent Asian, and 2 percent *other*. This particular decision wasn't something my friends, who were all non-Muslim, would understand. I had only a handful of Muslim peers, and even then, it was clear that we had very different priorities. Other fifteen-year-olds at school were worried about who was taking the most AP courses, who was invited to the upcoming party, or who was dating who. I had been thinking about it for weeks before I even reached out to Ms. Gottfried, but I knew I needed to talk through my feelings with someone older, someone with perspective. I didn't know if she—a Caucasian woman in her thirties—would comprehend the complexities of such a decision at my age. But there was no one else that I felt like I could confide in.

It started out as a secret that I kept to myself. I withdrew from the outside world and into my own mind, choosing to spend my lunches and breaks alone, weighing whether this was the right choice for me. I thought about how my family would feel. About what my friends would say. About how different parts of my life would change.

I walked past small offices with the names of different guidance counselors on each door until I found Ms. Gottfried's. Even though it was open, I knocked.

"Good morning."

"Gabbie. Hi. Come in, sit down, sit down," she said as she ushered me in. I settled into a chair on the other side of her desk, which was cluttered with folders labeled with the names of students from my grade. "I'm glad that you came to see me. Why don't you tell me what's been going on? What is the 'something drastic' that you've been thinking about?"

"Oh, I'm so sorry if that scared you. It's not what it sounds like," I said, pausing. "I don't think I've ever told you this before, but I'm Muslim."

"No, I don't think you have."

"Yeah, so, um, well...recently I've been thinking about wearing a headscarf as a daily way to practice my religion," I continued, looking down at my thumbs as I twiddled them. It was the first time I said it out loud.

"Oh, okay! Well, that is definitely not what I thought you were going to say. Tell me more about it. How long have you been thinking about this?" she asked.

"It's been a few weeks. There's this reality show, *All-American Muslim*, that came out in October. It follows a few Muslim families in Dearborn, Michigan," I started to say. Ms. Gottfried turned her computer screen toward me and typed the name into Google. She clicked on the first link and started to scroll.

"I didn't know about this. It seems really interesting," she said.

"Yeah, well, of course, it's becoming controversial because it shows Muslims in a positive light."

I remembered I didn't even want to watch *All-American Muslim* at first. It was my mom who suggested we watch it together. I thought it was going to be some boring documentary about the history of Muslims in the U.S.

"Anyways, so some of the women on the show wear a headscarf, and some don't," I explained. "The more episodes I watch, the more I realize that the women in the show who wear hijab don't lack anything in their lives because of it. They aren't restricted because of it. They actually have this additional layer to their lives, this closeness to our faith that I want to explore too."

"I can definitely understand that. It's such a brave decision to be thinking about," she said.

For her, she probably thought it was brave because no one at my high school had ever worn a hijab before, but I didn't feel brave. I was just following an internal compulsion—a pulling inside of me.

"Thanks," I murmured with a shy smile.

"In your email, you said you don't have anyone else to talk to about this. Why do you feel that way?" Ms. Gottfried asked.

In Islam, the choice to wear a hijab is a deeply personal journey. Contrary to popular misconceptions, it's not an act that is meant to be forced upon a woman. While I knew my family would never push me one way or the other, I thought there would be some expectation that I would wear the hijab once I brought it up. It wasn't something I could just talk about and then take back. And I didn't want it to just be an experiment, abandoned as my fascination with the idea faded.

Because of the respect I had developed for the hijab, I knew it would be a life-long commitment for me. So, I felt the decision had to solely come from me and remain uninfluenced by anyone around me—society at large, friends, and even family.

Religion had played a part in my upbringing, but I wouldn't have described my family as particularly devout. My grandparents had immigrated to the United States from Guyana in the seventies, and one of the unique things about the Indo-Caribbean community is the difference in religion within families. Some of my mother's extended family are Hindus and Jehovah's Witnesses, and my father's entire family practices either Christianity or Hinduism.

While I attended an Islamic school until second grade, my parents took me to classes every week where I learned to read the Qur'an, and we went to the masjid regularly during Ramadan, we also didn't pray five times a day and no one in my family wore a hijab. There was sometimes a picking-and-choosing of the practices that were observed, and even when we adhere to religious customs, we often did so without learning the purpose behind them—which is the reason I didn't understand why I had to wear a hijab when I entered a masjid or why some women wore it in public. Then, it was just a mark of religiosity to me. Eventually, my aunt became the first in our family to wear the hijab, but she made that choice in her early thirties when she was already married and had her first child. So even in my family, I didn't have peers who could grasp why I would wear one at my age or the nuances of such a decision.

I explained this to Ms. Gottfried.

"I see. I want you to know that you are not alone in this, even if no one else you know has gone through this in the same way before. Mrs. Greenberg is our school social worker, and I think it might be helpful for you to meet with her. This is definitely a big decision, and she can help you process all of your thoughts. How does that sound?" she replied.

"Yeah, that would be great. Thank you so much."

"You're welcome," she said as she filled out a pass for me to return to class. "Regardless of what you decide, this is all very commendable. And, Gabbie?"

"Yes."

"When you're ready, I think you should let your mom in. She'll understand."

I nodded and then started the long journey to my English classroom at the other end of the building.

When my parents, sister, and I settled in the dinette later that night, the usual dinner-time conversation took place.

"How was your day at school," my mom asked my sister and me.

"Good." I paused for a moment, thinking about whether to bring up my conversation with Ms. Gottfried. I shook the thought out of my mind. "Got a ninety-six on my trig test."

"That's excellent. Great job," she said.

"That's it? Where's the other four points?" my father replied, laughing at his classic immigrant dad joke.

❧

The following week, I met with Mrs. Greenberg—a Jewish woman in her early fifties—for the first time.

"What are the reasons that you want to wear the headscarf?" she asked.

"Aside from establishing a stronger connection to my faith, I think it's to discover who I am without my hair."

"What do you mean?" she replied, peering at me with interest.

"About a year ago, I started going to a women's class at the mosque near my house. One day, the teacher explained that wearing the hijab allows you to be valued for who you are as a person, your inner qualities and talents, rather than what you look like," I said, pausing.

Mrs. Greenberg nodded.

"I knew that the hijab was about modesty, but it was the first time that I thought about it *that* way. And recently, I realized that my hair is starting to become a defining part of my identity."

"How so?"

"Ever since I was a baby, there's been this obsession with my hair. It's always been thick and jet black, like this." I said, pinching a few strands between my fingers. "Not many people in my family have hair this thick, not even my sister or my mom. And most of the time, when I wake up for school, I don't even need to brush it. It looks like this without me having to do anything. You know, when I walked in the door this morning, my friends complimented my hair before they even said good morning."

"Do you think that's a bad thing?"

"No, don't get me wrong. I appreciate the compliments. But it's the first thing people notice—it's always been the special thing about me. It's even developed into an obsession of my own. I only let one lady at the salon cut my hair, and it has to be done in a very specific way. Long layers to the middle of my back with side bangs parted to the left. When I heard what the teacher said at the class, it made me wonder what I would discover about myself if I took my hair out of the equation."

"What do you think you'll find?" Mrs. Greenberg asked.

"I'm not sure I'll ever know until I try."

I would meet with Mrs. Greenberg over the course of the next seven months until the summer break, weighing the pros and cons of this decision and assessing the right time to start telling the people closest to me.

A few months later, my aunt picked my mom and me up to attend the women's class at the local masjid, as we did every Saturday morning. It was from this class that both my mother and I took up a deeper interest in Islam. The drives home afterward were reserved for a recap discussion of the week's topic, the latest news among the class's volunteer group we were a part of, and the occasional update on the most recent family drama.

"You know, you can't just practice some things and not others," my aunt said. She believed in more of an all-or-nothing approach.

This was one in a series of conversations in which she and my mother would encourage me to stop listening to music—in adherence to one of the more conservative guidelines in Islam. At this point in my life, earbuds were always in my ears, so much so that I would get in trouble for not hearing my mother when she'd call me down for dinner.

My mind flashed back to my conversations with Mrs. Greenberg. Maybe I wasn't ready to give up music, but I *was* thinking about other ways to be more connected to my faith.

How can I expect them to know that? I've never told them, I thought.

Should I tell them? Am I ready? I wasn't sure.

Once I say it, there's no going back. But the words came bursting out of my mouth anyway.

"Well, I've been thinking about starting to wear the hijab."

I let out a deep breath and watched their expressions as they looked back at me, registering my words. The car was silent.

The weeks that followed my spontaneous outburst were spent in conversations with the closest people in my life, getting their take on what I had been mulling over in my head for months. My friends' responses were the most predictable.

"So your parents are making you do this?" they asked when I finally told them.

"No. It was something I decided I wanted to do on my own," I replied.

"What? Why would you want to cover your hair? It's so beautiful," one of them responded, sorely missing the point.

Only one friend—the first one I made at school, a devout Catholic girl from a Malayalee family—understood without me having to explain.

As the discussions with my family continued, it was their reactions that I became more and more surprised by.

My aunt was happy at the prospect of no longer being the only hijabi in our family. But she also made sure that I had thought my decision through.

"Are you sure about this?" she asked. "If you aren't, that's okay too."

Years later, she would tell me that, at the time, she worried that I may have been too young to make such a big commitment.

My grandparents on my mother's side—who are Muslim and who I thought would persuade me toward the traditional choice—seemed ambivalent, but ultimately, they voiced their support for whatever decision I made.

"Sure, if that's something that you want to do," they said, one echoing the other after some silence.

And then there were my parents, who caught me completely off-guard.

"Your dad and I think you should wait until college. Doing this in the middle of high school will be hard. Everyone knows you one way, and kids are mean. When you start college, it's easier to make a big change like this. They'll only ever have to know you one way, whatever way you choose," my mother said as we had lunch together at an Olive Garden.

"I don't want to wait until then. Who knows what will happen over the next two years?" I replied.

But I knew exactly what would happen. I would lose my nerve. Or, some guy would come walking into my life and I'd get distracted.

I had been so worried that if I told my family before I was sure of what I wanted, they would encourage me to wear the hijab. And maybe it would have been like that if we didn't live in a post-9/11 world. But instead, I was met with apprehension that stemmed from a place of protection, making sure that I knew the many ways my life would be impacted by this decision and that it wouldn't be an easy path to travel.

But by explaining the reasons why I wanted to wear the hijab in each exchange, my conviction only grew stronger. If I wanted to do it, I had to do it now.

At the end of my sophomore year, I started volunteering at the Long Island Children's Museum to keep busy for the summer. July 2, 2012, was my first day—the end of one chapter and the beginning of another in more than one way.

But it started out as a morning like any other.

"Gabbie, you have ten minutes to get ready or you'll be late," my mother called.

While rubbing the sleep from my eyes, I pushed myself off my bed and stumbled to the bathroom to brush my teeth. Back in my room, I pulled on a pair of jeans and a black blouse.

Then I grabbed an under-cap from my drawer and placed it on my head. Next, I found my favorite purple scarf and lined it up so the under-cap could create a border like I had seen countless times in tutorials on YouTube. Looking in the mirror, I brought the two sides of the fabric together at the nape of my neck and pinned it. Then I wrapped each piece to cover my neck and the top of my chest.

I threw my bag over my shoulder and bounded down the steps into the kitchen, where my mother was.

"Your dad is already in the car," she said, handing me a cup of tea and my lunch for the day. Then she stopped for a moment to look at me. "Ready?"

"Ready."

being

The following story contains sensitive material that
may be triggering for trauma survivors and those who
suffer from mental health conditions. Suicidal ideation
is a topic mentioned in this author's moment.

If you feel triggered, please know there are resources to support you.

U.S. National Suicide Hotline
1-800-273-8255

THE WHISPERING OF THE JINN

BY M.K. ANSARI

"HOW WOULD YOUR FRIENDS DESCRIBE YOU?" Dr. Nayak asked me.

"Intense," I replied, holding her gaze. She looked like yet another uppity Silicon Valley auntie in her beige cashmere blazer, her hair in a French twist. But she wasn't an auntie—at least not within these bare walls.

I rolled up the sleeves of my blue scrubs. Dr. Nayak examined my arm.

"Those are just scratches," she whispered.

"There were sharper things in the house," I said, leaning back calmly in my plastic chair. "In fact, I could kill myself with any object in this room."

My eyes darted from side to side to take in my surroundings.

"You guys have done a fantastic job," I said. "This place is suicide proof."

"Are you a comedian?" she asked, smiling calmly. *She thinks I'm here doing character research*, I thought. I didn't know what to tell her. Do I tell her I was a successful Silicon Valley corporate lawyer with a seemingly perfect life? Do I explain to her that somehow I found myself suicidal after I'd won a screenwriting contest? I leaned forward, folding my hands on the table.

"You're good at this," I said. "I'm a comedy screenwriter. I won a few contests in Hollywood and then spiraled into depression."

Or was that all a dream, a delusion? The line between the real and the imaginary had become blurred in the last month. If I saw a tree, I questioned its existence. If someone gave me a compliment, I questioned its motive.

"Do you know what it feels like to know things that only you know?" I asked Dr. Nayak.

"You hear voices?"

"No, that's clair*audience*. And clair*voyance* is when you see visions. I'm clair*cognizant*," I said, "I *know* things. I read minds. I smell people's fears."

In moments of mental disconnect, time moved more slowly. I could see every movement of a person's face and hear even the most subtle inflections in their voice.

"You believe you are part of something secret or special?" she asked.

I shrugged.

"Did you experience abuse as a child?" she continued.

Before I could answer, Dylan in the room next to us started hitting his head on the wall.

Thud. Thud. THUD!

"CODE GREEN!" the nurses outside screamed in panic. Dr. Nayak fled out of the room.

"Dylan, stop or we'll send you to the third floor. You remember what they do there?" I heard the orderly say.

Dr. Nayak walked back into my room, not a single silky gray strand of hair out of place.

"First thing tomorrow, I'm going to have you moved downstairs, with the other—"

"Sociopaths?" I said with a wink.

Downstairs was a sedative junkie's dream. They gave us sedatives for sleep, sedatives for headaches, even sedatives for PMS. Still, it wasn't a dreamland. This floor didn't have head-banging Dylan or old lady Bessie throwing grapes at the nurses, but it was a prison of its own.

My roommate, Bella, cried herself to sleep. She was schizoaffective. That's when you have schizophrenic traits layered on top of bipolar mood swings, like a trifle of neuroses.

"My fiancé's cheating. He didn't pick up."

"Maybe he was in the shower," I mumbled. Bella started crying again. I stumbled out of my bed and sat on hers. Bella looked like a vulnerable child with her wispy silhouette and her slumped posture. "How old are you?"

"Twenty," she replied.

"Your twenties are a confusing time." Paranoia, I would find out, was part of something called "psychosis," often found in schizophrenia, schizoaffective disorder, and bipolar disorders.

"Were your twenties bad?" Bella said as she sat up.

"Yeah."

Ancient echoes of decades-old self-talk flooded back to me: *Everyone hates me. They're all talking about me. I should just stand in front of a subway train.* I never stood in front of the train. Instead, I had marched myself to the emergency room at age nineteen and was diagnosed with depression. I had to flush my meds down the toilet when Mom found them.

"Inn counselors-shounselors ko dehkna chordo!" she had scolded. "Stop seeing counselors! Who will marry you if they think you're mental?"

So, instead of psychiatry, I leaned on the clergy and became increasingly religious. "Drink this and the waswasa—the whispering of the jinn—will leave you," the Imam had told me, handing me a plastic soda bottle filled with holy water. I drank, but the jinn never left. Their hateful whispers consumed me and dared me to slice my wrists. I looked for answers in religious texts and studied mystical rules of jadoo—black magic—and the unseen realms. I had memorized all of the signs of the apocalypse and knew the exact date of the Day of Judgement, believing that religious knowledge would save my damned soul and stop the voices—the satanic whispers, the waswasa. The detached mind is brilliant at creating magical strings of theory from unrelated phenomena. That's what psychosis is—a reality distortion field.

I became convinced that my mom was possessed by a jinn. It was the only explanation for my traumatic childhood. As she slept, I sprinkled holy water on her, but no jinn came flying out. Instead, a hand with a chappal did and she cried for an hour about how Allah had given her ungrateful kids.

"Checks!" The nurse barged open the wardroom door. I rushed to my bed. My sedative began to turn the room in circles as I fell asleep to Bella's soft whimpers.

❧

"Tell me about your parents," Dr. Nayak said the next day as she sat across the desk from me.

"Mom wanted me to get a graduate degree but also marry young, effortlessly raise kids, throw lavish parties..."

"And you did all of that."

"I'm almost forty. I have two kids, a high-paying job, a rich and doting husband, and I know how to cook. And yet I'm here, after a suicide attempt. I'm tired of playing the part of the perfect Pakistani girl."

"So what led you here then?"

"I did what I was supposed to...I did what my parents wanted me to do. And then, I started following my dream, Hollywood," I said.

"And the minute you got close to your own dream, you tried to commit suicide," Dr. Nayak said as she looked at me with concern.

"My mom never understood me. She never gave me space. She tried so hard to get inside my head to shape it to fit her playbook," I said.

The fragrance of humid Canadian summers and memories of my mom dressing me like a doll for wedding after wedding came flooding back to me. Meddling aunties would monopolize the center tables, chewing their paan, pairing off the eligible bachelors with the "Good Girls." But Good Girls didn't go to law school and live in dorms. They harangued me at each event. "We forbid you to attend law school! Nobody proposes to lawyers," Mom said.

"How did you convince your parents to send you to law school?" Dr. Nayak asked.

"I broke Mom's fine china," I replied.

The plate had flown across the kitchen, my twenty-one-year-old self in the calm eye of a hurricane of cups, plates, and saucers. The doctor wrote in her notepad as I spoke.

"She thinks you're wack," the voices whispered.

"You think I'm a sociopath, don't you?" I asked.

Dr. Nayak looked at me serenely.

"Everything is a spectrum and we're all on it."

❧

Later that night, as my sedatives were melting into my blood, I heard a familiar voice in the darkness.

"He called," Bella whispered.

I propped my head on my hand and faced her.

"He was in the shower," Bella said, "How did you know? Are you psychic?"

"I have eighteen years more life experience than you."

"I'm so lost," Bella said with a heavy sigh. "I don't know if my fiancé loves me. I don't know if I have a future. I don't even know what to major in!"

Bella began to sob as I sat up in my bed, hugging my pillow.

"How did you know what you wanted to do?" she asked me.

"I learned how to silence the whispers."

"You're the first person who's ever understood me." Bella rolled over as she drifted off. "All I've ever wanted is to be understood."

"That's what I want too," I said. My eyes closed until the sun rose the next morning.

"Wallet, phone." I grabbed the items from the nurse as she took them out of a transparent plastic bag and checked off her list.

Bella was curled up in her bed, crying. "I'm not going to be okay without you," she said as tears streamed down her face. "I want to die."

I've only known you for a few days, I thought, but I also knew that psychosis could blur one's reality on relationships. In her mind, I was her new big sister. An hour ago, she'd told the cleaning lady that she was her "hospital mother" and had asked for her phone number.

❧

Dr. Nayak walked into the room.

"So what's the verdict?" I asked. "Am I a sociopath? Schizophrenic?"

"You have depression with borderline traits—"

"—traits?" I interrupted.

"We're all on a spectrum. In the past, borderline was considered the female version of sociopathy. But a sociopath has no empathy. You're an empath, a healer. You absorb people's pain and their expectations," she smiled at me. "I'm prescribing an antidepressant."

"Is that all?" I asked.

"In three days, there was only so much history I could get. You're a very nuanced person. If there's more to your diagnosis, the antidepressant will reveal it. Follow up with your outside psychiatrist and..."

"Yes?" I waited.

"Don't stop the creative work," she said smiling. "Where can I watch your films or shows?"

I sighed.

"When I make it to the big screen, I'll find a way to get the word out to you."

Then she was gone, seventy-two hours after she arrived. Auntie Nayak.

❧

A week later, the aftershocks came. The antidepressants made me paranoid, suicidal, and afraid. I was afraid to leave the house—afraid to leave my bed. I was even afraid that my own kids would try to harm me. I had hallucinations. I heard trumpets that weren't playing. I saw shadows move in the darkness. My primary care doctor immediately made me stop taking antidepressants.

"Your episodes have both manic and depressive features," my new psychiatrist said. "Antidepressants treat depression but make you manic. Somebody with your life shouldn't be this depressed. Yet, you get depressed or manic every time you accomplish anything."

"Why do achievements make me spiral?" I asked.

"Your brain chemistry fights happiness like it's an invader. And you also have underlying psychological reasons. You simply don't believe you deserve to win."

It's been six months since the psychiatric hospital. My doctor realized I needed medication after I charted my every mood for two months. That's where he saw that I live in a world of perpetual darkness, despite the illusion of perfection that others see when they look at me. He finally saw past my mask. We monitor my mental state in a daily calendar until I'm back to my baseline self, but I'm not sure what baseline looks like anymore. I only just started medication, and even that is an ongoing, trial-and-error process because my diagnosis isn't easy for anyone—not even a trained psychiatrist—to understand. What are the whispers? Are they mania? Are they a delusion? A hallucination? Or am I just a misunderstood psychic? My psychiatrist refuses to attach labels.

"Mental health is a spectrum, and we're all on it," he said.

I don't have all the answers. But I know one thing—my jinn still whispers.

The following story contains sensitive material that may be triggering for trauma survivors and those who suffer from mental health conditions. Infant mortality is a topic mentioned in this author's moment.

If you feel triggered, please know there are resources to support you.

POOR OBSTETRIC OUTCOME

BY POOJA PATEL

I LAY IN A HOSPITAL BED IN ATLANTA, catatonic with grief. My baby was dead, cold, and lifeless in a glass bassinet at my side.

After my son Sohan's death, I asked my Bengali-American OB-GYN friend what she thought my chances were of successfully carrying a child. Over the phone, her hesitation was palpable.

"Pooja, your chances of having a safe pregnancy are slim, and you will be labeled by doctors as a patient with poor obstetric outcome."

Geez, I thought. *Poor obstetric outcome. P.O.O. That's real shitty.*

Through years of infertility, miscarriages, and the death of my child, I am learning what grief truly means. Oddly, sometimes grief means laughter. It means being in the hospital talking about an Indian open defecation documentary your friend watched and then suddenly remembering your kid is dead. It means deciding that, if you were an animal, you would be a panda because they, too, have a soft belly and under-eye circles and rely on a team of experts to get pregnant. Grief means being at a funeral home and only focusing on the gaudy purple carpet and colorful bowtie of the funeral director. It means realizing that, for the first time, you are not there for the many Indian funerals this building has held, but for the preparation of *your* baby's funeral. It means seeing an Indian-American counselor you assume will be familiar with the family dynamics of loss in South Asian communities, but all you can focus on is how she looks like an aunty you know, and you wonder if she'll notice how many Starbursts you ate from her candy jar while waiting. Grief means watching *Shrek the Third* and feeling jealous of Fiona for getting pregnant when you can't. That green bitch.

My husband, Akit, and I are approaching eight years trying for a live birth. A mere year into our marriage, and blissfully unaware of what our future held, Akit came home frazzled and embarrassed.

"I was in the car with dad on the way to Best Buy. He told me Serena and Jamal are having fertility issues because Jamal has a sperm issue, and then he asked me if my sperm is okay."

"What the hell? What did you tell him?" I asked, stifling laughter.

"I told him my sperm is fine, so let's never talk about my sperm again. But he kept pressing me and telling me not to wait to have kids."

We laughed that, growing up, Indians never discuss pee-pees and hoohas or sexual health with their kids but are blunt enough to bring it up so soon after marriage. I think back to that conversation often. I know it must have been so uncomfortable for my father-in-law to mention this to my husband, but he cared enough to warn us.

I later discussed that conversation with Serena and Jamal after we began encountering our own fertility issues. Serena told me that she had to explain basic reproductive health to her Indian in-laws, who didn't understand that men can have fertility problems too and that her husband's sperm was not reaching her egg to fertilize it. *How can people from a country with overpopulation issues not understand how babies are made?* I wondered.

We had to navigate many awkward conversations with aunties and uncles prying into when we were going to have kids. At my older sister's baby shower, Anita aunty approached my mother.

"Is Pooja pregnant, too?"

"If she is expecting, she hasn't said anything to us, but I don't think she is."

After the guests left, I helped my mom clean up.

"Anita aunty was asking if you were expecting, but I told her I didn't know."

She stared at me expectantly with a gleam of hope in her eye.

"No, mummy, I am not pregnant. Just fat."

In our frustration, Akit and I came up with a game plan. The next time someone asked us when we'll have kids, we would loudly announce:

"Aunty wants us to have SEX! Where is there a free bedroom?"

But rather than muster the courage to scream that in their faces, we would shift uncomfortably and give a canned answer.

"When the time is right."

Soon after those awkward conversations, we finally decided we were ready to grow our family. However, I have PCOS—a disease that causes anovulation and commonly afflicts South Asians. PCOS leaves one fat and infertile with facial hair that could rival Daler Mehndi. We tried for a short time on our own before moving on to fertility treatments.

As we entered the clinic, we were immediately struck, gobsmacked, and stunned—the entire waiting room was packed with other South Asians. We thought we were alone, but we were suffering in silence with couples who looked just like us.

One year after starting fertility treatments, I was pregnant and ecstatic. We went to our initial ultrasound visit eager to see the first glimpse of our son or daughter. The cold and dark room grew unnervingly quiet before the ultrasound technician said:

"Let me get the doctor."

My husband, a physician, knew something was wrong.

The doctor entered and turned the ultrasound monitor to face him so we couldn't see the screen. He asked me to stay very still and hold my breath. I felt the adrenaline coursing through me as I attempted to follow his instructions. His expression was stoic.

"I see a faint heartbeat, but the gestational sac is not measuring appropriately. I want to see you back in a week, but there is a high likelihood this pregnancy will result in miscarriage."

I quietly sobbed as the nurse and ultrasound technician comforted me.

"I am so sorry, Dr. Patel," the nurse whispered to my husband as they left the room. I realized at that moment, he wasn't a doctor—he was a grieving father. My heart sank further.

"We have some news," my husband later told our parents over the phone, while I lay in bed, crying. "Pooja was pregnant, but we just found out that the baby stopped growing. The doctor has scheduled a D&C procedure to remove the fetal tissue. Our baby."

My mother flew to our home in Texas, where we were living at the time, to console me.

"These things happen. It is nature's way. I knew a woman in India who would wake up covered in blood during her pregnancies, and she had a kid at forty-five. You are still very young and have so much time. Don't stress. It is not good for your health."

"No, Mummy. You don't understand how hard it was for me to even get pregnant. We needed fertility treatments. What if this is just the beginning of worse things to come?" I said to her.

Several weeks after the procedure, we received the medical report on our baby's tissue sample. While my husband was at work, I opened the envelope trembling, scared of what it would say. I scanned the paper, barely registering what I was reading, and then I saw it:

Sex: Male.

So our baby was a boy. It was the first of many times we would learn something about our child through an autopsy report.

Our parents quietly told us about the many people they knew whose children had to go through IUI, IVF, and ovulation induction to have children. I joined private social media groups for couples trying to conceive. I learned all the acronyms and lingo associated with the process as I excitedly waited for my next BFP (big fat positive) pregnancy test as we continued TTC (trying to conceive).

Over the next few years, I would get pregnant again, both naturally and as a result of fertility treatments. None of the pregnancies would result in a live birth. Doctors were confused, and so were we. Family members told us we should try various pujas, wear certain stones, and consult with pandits about our horoscopes to find out why none of my pregnancies resulted in a healthy child.

The curse was yet to be broken. Rather than holding a chubby little Parle-G baby in our arms, we were bereaved parents mourning the loss of our son. After his death, our families had very different responses. My North Indian Brahmin mother insisted on a four-hour puja, complete with a gigantic yellow sapphire ring like the *Avengers: Endgame* infinity stone.

My side of the family openly discussed and remembered our son on a regular basis. We planted trees together in his honor, built a keepsake box, and laughed remembering what a jungli baby he was in utero. My white brothers-in-law sat through the prayer ceremony and openly cried, bereft with the loss of their nephew. Theirs is an open grief.

The response of my husband's Gujarati family was one of stoicism and emotional fortitude bred from a history of overcoming hardships and starting from scratch. While still in the hospital recovering from my C-section, they started planning the next steps. They told us about the surrogacy commercials they had seen on Indian TV and offered financial support if we pursued it as a safer path to parenthood. They even encouraged us to have two surrogates, if need be. Theirs is a pragmatic grief.

At times, we have been frustrated with our families, but ultimately, we know that each side offers a different type of strength.

As we slowly shared our story outside of our family, many of our friends privately told us about their fertility struggles. We were all seeing the same doctor and had somehow never run into one another at the clinic. My husband and I did a rough estimation and found that close to 60 percent of our friends had undergone some form of fertility treatment. Our doctor told us younger and younger couples are struggling to conceive, and South Asians are a commonly affected group. We thought back to the packed waiting room choking with couples who looked like us and realized this was no surprise. Yet, it took our son dying for people to open up about their onerous journeys to parenthood.

～&

At home in Atlanta, Georgia, I brushed my hand along the scar on my lower belly, a vestige of what once was and what I can no longer safely do. For the next thirty seconds, a river of tears made its way down my cheek. This is how I cry now—suddenly and quickly. As the tears dried, I considered our next step for putting our proverbial naan in someone else's tandoori oven to bake for nine months.

I felt overwhelmed but determined, so I opened my computer and logged in to Facebook to start my post:

Hi, my name is Pooja. On December 28, my husband and I lost our son after an emergency C-section. We are looking for a gestational carrier to help grow our family . . .

DARK AND LOVELY

BY APOORVA VERGHESE

DURING MY CHILDHOOD VISITS TO INDIA, I was always careful to cover myself in long sleeves and jeans. Under the blistering sun, men my grandfather's age would walk around shirtless and unabashed, but no degree of heat could force me to expose my dark, sticky, sweat-glistened skin.

"Karappi," my relatives always murmured the second they picked us up from the airport. Karappi means dark girl. The pity in their tones did the work of translation for me. Karappi, ugly girl.

During those long, lazy summers, my sister and I spent most of our days sprawled across my grandparents' divan, watching soap operas on the ancient, staticky TV. Every few minutes, a dramatic family feud would be interrupted by an advertisement. Usually, I didn't pay the commercials any attention, except perhaps to laugh at a strange new marketing tactic. But one caught my eye—an ad for Fair & Lovely, India's leading skin-bleaching cream.

It was always easy to identify these ads. They'd employ the same sickly sweet music and always featured a sad, dark-skinned girl who tries the cream and then suddenly becomes marriage material. Most of all, though, I could always identify these ads by how harshly *white* they were, from the skin of the actors to the fluorescent lighting to the backdrops. Everything was so white that I struggled to make out their faces. The takeaway couldn't be clearer: White was right. White was beautiful. Dark was ugly. I was ugly.

I did my best to ignore these ads when they came on, burrowing my head in a book or turning over to talk to my sister. They typically needled at me, but one day, when I was seven years old, the needle pierced through my skin, pushed in deep, and drew blood.

That day, the face of my childhood hero appeared in the bright white ad. Shah Rukh Khan, or as I knew him, Raj—my Raj—the person who had won my heart with his mandolin-strumming and feathered cap in the iconic film, *Dilwale Dulhania Le Jayenge*. My sister and I used to watch *DDLJ* religiously, memorizing dialogue and song lyrics, even though neither of us knew Hindi.

Raj—the charming, mischievous hero from the diaspora—represented our relationship with India. Growing up in America, alienated from our homeland, both of us longed to be more in touch with our culture. Bollywood became a stand-in for our heritage. We fell in love with on-screen characters, we quoted dialogue to each other without ever knowing the meaning of our words—as most of our old VHS tapes didn't have English subtitles. Sometimes, our dad would sit with us and explain the stories and lines to us, but we preferred to make up our own. Every once in a while, usually during a particularly charged scene, I'd lean over to my sister and whisper:

"What's happening now?"

Even though our age gap was only four years, my sister, so self-assured at eleven years old, was the one I trusted with these translations—her word was always gospel for me.

"They're falling in love," she would respond authoritatively, smirking, her legs dangling off the armrests.

That was her response to everything.

Despite not knowing Hindi, she was right the majority of the time. That's just how the movies we watched worked. Handsome boys and beautiful girls met, flirted, and fell in love. *DDLJ* was even dearer to me because the pretty girl in question, Kajol, was an actress many people told me I resembled. The silly comparison—one most likely made to many little Indian girls—meant the world to me. It not only meant that I looked like Kajol but that I looked like a girl a handsome boy would fall in love with. A girl who *Raj* would fall for.

So that day, when Raj's face popped up in the commercial that had haunted me for years, I felt a strange, strangling sensation in my throat. *Why was my Raj telling me I had to be white?*

For some reason, Raj's endorsement of Fair & Lovely hit harder than my relatives' callous comments. I could brush those off, chalking them up to cultural differences or generational gaps. But, *this* betrayal stung in a deeper, more visceral way. I felt worse than ugly, I felt unlovable. My skin started to itch. I longed to scratch it off, to scrub off the charcoal coating of my body and emerge pure—brighter and whiter. For the first time, I started to buy into the twisted narrative of Fair & Lovely ads. Perhaps, to win the love of someone like Raj, I would have to change myself. The hard seed of a plan formed in my mind, and, two weeks later, on the day before we left India, I took action.

We went on our annual shopping spree, stocking up on all the uniquely Indian snacks we wouldn't be able to buy back home in the States. From Maggi noodles to Magic Masala chips, our haul was impressive. Then, in the midst of the hustle and bustle of the family expedition, I snuck away.

While they hunted for Cadbury chocolate, I headed to the beauty aisle, perusing hand lotions and hair dyes before hitting gold—a shelf full of slim, pink and white tubes of Fair & Lovely. I felt a strange magnetic attraction toward the display. I grabbed a tube, managed to slip it into the overflowing shopping cart unnoticed, and secretly celebrated my victory. This time tomorrow, I convinced myself, I would be unrecognizable. Scrubbed clean and white. I would finally be beautiful.

It was a fleeting joy, however, cut short as we rolled the cart to the trolley and unloaded its contents onto the checkout counter. Immediately, my mother's eagle eyes spotted the outlier among our snacks. She grabbed the Fair & Lovely tube, her eyes wide and sad.

"What is this?" she asked me and my sister, who instantly denied taking the product. My mother looked at me, pointedly. "Why would you buy something like this?"

I burned with embarrassment, my skin feeling slimy under her gaze.

"Oh, I just wanted to try it," I said flippantly, fiddling with my hair to hide how badly I wanted to sink into the floor.

My mother's mouth was set in a tight line. *I hope she doesn't make me put it back*, I thought.

Looking at each other as we stood not knowing what to say, my eyes focused on her skin. It was light but just golden enough not to burn red from the glare of the sun. Even my mother's name, Jessy, evoked whiteness—she is a fair and lovely dream. I have her eyes, brain, and tendency to get lost in daydreams. But my dark skin gave me no claim to her beauty.

Growing up, neither of my parents ever let us feel the sting of colorism at home. But in India, my mother couldn't stop relatives from comparing her lightness to her children's darkness. When family members told my sister and me not to play outside in the sun, for fear we would become darker, she felt the pain of their comments almost as intensely as we did. She tried so hard to shield us from harmful beauty standards that to see me buying this bottle likely felt like a personal failure.

"Fine," my mother said coldly, after a long pause, not wanting to make a scene in front of the whole store.

"Don't worry, I don't really care. I'm just curious. I want to test it and see if it'll work," I said, laughing, feeling relieved that I'd get to keep it.

My sister laughed too, but, unlike mine, hers was genuine.

"Well, the cream is white, so it should work—as long as you don't rub it in, you'll be white too."

My sister was not immune to these beauty standards, but at the time, she was certainly stronger than me. It was as though her entire body was a living metaphor. A few years prior, she had gone through a phase of killing her curls by straightening them. But within a day, you could see her hair fighting back as the ends twisted and her roots lifted. Eventually, she stopped straightening her hair all together and accepted the beauty of her natural look. She understood the hollow danger of the fairness ideal more clearly than I did. She was in the process of actively striking down the dangerous beauty norms embedded within us—a journey I had yet to start.

My mother was not amused, just disappointed. In herself, in me, in India. Still, she knew there was no point in trying to stop me. Driving home, I was so excited to open that tube that all those indulgent wishes of sugar and salt melted away. As we carried the bags, I dove straight for the lotion.

"I'll be back!" I yelled over my shoulder.

I slipped into the bedroom and climbed on top of the hard mattress, placing the tube squarely in front of me. Half of me wanted to grab it and squeeze it all over myself. But part of me was plagued with concerns. *What about the chemicals? What if I flush red instead of white? What if it just doesn't work? Why do I want it to work?*

I pushed the thoughts aside. And with chipped-polished nails, I opened the tube and covered my arms and legs with its sticky solution until they were fully saturated.

❧

The next morning, I woke up with some expectations of an overnight transformation. I threw off the covers, quickly got out of bed, and walked over to the mirror in my room, where I discovered that I was still the exact same shade of brown.

No change.

The disillusionment pained me, but more than anything, I was frustrated. Frustrated that the cream didn't work instantly—frustrated at myself for thinking it would.

I turned around, picked up the tube, and immediately threw it in the trash.

❧

I didn't know it then, but this moment launched me on a journey to self-love that has been slow, steady, and ongoing. It would be years until I finally confronted the question at the core of this lifelong battle: *Why do we even care about fairness?*

I, like so many susceptible children, had been socialized to believe that beauty is binary and narrow. Fair is lovely, and dark is ugly.

This summer, I plan to wear T-shirts and shorts under the blazing Indian sun. My skin will catch my eye, glazed with humidity. I will wear it proudly. Dark and lovely.

The following story contains sensitive material that may be triggering for trauma survivors and those who suffer from mental health conditions. Suicide, suicidal ideation, and murder are some of the topics mentioned in this author's moment.

If you feel triggered, please know there are resources to support you.

U.S. National Suicide Hotline
1-800-273-8255

SURVIVING SUICIDE

BY SUBRINA SINGH

DATES HAVE ALWAYS BEEN IMPORTANT TO ME. I've remembered and marked each meaningful date in my life since my diagnosis with bipolar disorder on October 26, 2006. Still, I cannot recall the date in July when I lay in bed, crying and screaming, thinking to myself, *How unfair for her to die—if anyone had to die, it should have been me.* I was already sick and had already suffered. There had been so many days since I was fourteen that I had prayed for death, so why not me?

At that moment, I made a decision. It was a choice I had debated for years.

I reached over to my nightstand, opened my drawer, and searched for my medication. I emptied the bottle of pills into my hand and gulped them down with a bottle of water. I turned off the lights and waited for my peaceful ending. My eyes closed, but all I could feel was the hair on my body rising and my heart racing.

Moments later, I realized I had failed, and as I sat in the ambulance, all I thought about was how *badly* I had failed.

I knew I would see my parents in the emergency room. What would they say? I could already feel their judgment. One more disappointment. The problem was I didn't regret taking the pills. I was more upset that my overdose wasn't successful. After hours in the emergency room, I was officially committed.

I hated hospitals. They reeked of rubbing alcohol and disease. I cried and begged my parents to do something, hoping they could find a way to just take me home, but it was out of their hands. As I was escorted to the psych ward, I kept my head down, letting the tears roll off my face. I could not bear to make eye contact with my family members as I left them—I was overcome with shame. I knew I would never be able to take back the heartache I had inflicted on them.

Butterflies filled my stomach. I didn't have an idea of what to expect. I wasn't supposed to end up here. I should have been dead. The long hallways led to rooms filled with patients, but I felt entirely alone.

The doctors did not pump my stomach, but I was on suicide watch. Yet somehow, I was able to charm my way out of the hospital without a full seventy-two-hour stay, which at the time seemed like quite an accomplishment. But the problem was that I was still extremely suicidal. My grief and sadness consumed me in every way, but due to my mental illness, I had perfected my façade. I convinced everyone that I was better, and some days, I even bought my own story.

I abided by my wellness and safety plan and attended psychiatry and therapy sessions. In those forty-five minutes, I vented and spoke my truth, convincing myself it was helping, but I still cried myself to sleep at night. Sometimes, I sat in my car and screamed with tears rolling down my eyes in the parking lot of CVS. But all my family could see was that I was going to school and appeared to be excelling. My mask was so perfect that it was impossible to see what lay beneath.

You see, my suicide attempt was years in the making. I had planned, brainstormed, and made lists without people ever suspecting that anything was wrong. But every person has a breaking point. I spent years questioning my purpose and wondering what my life was worth, but my catalyst was the day the world as I knew it changed.

March 18, 2012, was the day my glass house shattered, the day hatred, cruelty, and gun violence took my eldest sister. I can recall bits and pieces of the events from that week, but most of it was a blur.

I often think back to that Sunday morning. Closing my eyes, I remember texting and calling my sister, not knowing that her cell phone had already been taken as evidence by the police.

I love you. See you soon. Those were the last words I sent her, thinking I would see her again. Meanwhile, her body was being processed for an autopsy.

I arrived home and knew something was off immediately. I sat on the floor of our den, screaming as they told me that my sister had been murdered. It was the same room I had last embraced her. This could not be real.

My mom had already contacted my psychiatrist, unsure of how I would react to the news. She was prepared with sedatives, which I took eagerly, hoping to numb the feeling of emptiness I felt inside my heart.

My house was like a revolving door bringing in people who attempted to console us. My knees were weak as I leaned on guests, who hugged me and murmured condolences:

"I'm so sorry for your loss. My thoughts are with you during this difficult time."

I could feel the awkwardness and tension behind these statements. There were no right words. There were no words at all.

The next day, I sunk deeper into this reality. The car slowly drove down the crowded Queens, New York, street, tears filling my eyes as I slouched down in the front seat. Under different circumstances, it would have been a beautiful day—the trees had just begun to sprout new leaves.

I tried to remain composed, but I began bawling as we approached her house. It was the first time I had seen it since the shooting, and I had only one thought in my mind: *My sister took her last breath on that porch, on that seat.* Most of the blood had been washed out from the driveway, but I could still see dark red stains. It took a second, but then it hit me. *Those weren't just stains—they were remnants of her.*

As I walked up to my sister's house, I saw the bullet holes dotting the fence. I outlined each hole with my finger. It was then I realized the level of violence and injustice that my family had suffered.

She had still been on maternity leave after giving birth to her second son and was just shy of her fortieth birthday when she was killed. I always admired her vivacious spirit and her "Forever Young" mindset.

As we prepared for her wake and funeral services, we spent time in her home trying to celebrate her life with friends and family in the backyard, dancing and playing dominoes. From the outside, it probably looked more like a Queens house party than a wake, but it was exactly what she would have wanted.

"When I die, I don't want people to sit there and cry. I want people to play dominoes and cards. I don't want bhajans—I want music and a DJ. I want people dancing," she once told me at a family funeral.

It was all so surreal—I kept waiting for her to walk through the door, laughing, ending this nightmare.

I was so heavily medicated that I floated through the week in a haze, but I vividly remember the first time I saw her body lying cold and lifeless in a coffin. Her beautiful auburn curls framed the face I had admired my entire life. I touched her cautiously, and as I felt her frigid skin, tears came to my eyes. At that moment, I fully realized for the first time that my eldest sister had been called home. Her body laid before me, but it was just a body.

What gives a man the right to take a life? Only God has that right.

All I could do was cry.

With vibrant tassa drums, her favorite music blasting from speakers, and loved ones paying their respects as they toasted her photo with beer bottles, we honored her life in the most unorthodox way.

She wanted her life to be celebrated, not mourned. Still, I didn't know what to celebrate. I often snuck away to cry in the bathroom. There was not enough medication in the world that could take away the grief that consumed me. My eldest sister was like a second mom. She passed on her wisdom, often telling me stories of her own adolescence. She always encouraged me to make the best of any bad situation.

After I received my diagnosis, she became my confidante in a new way. She always asked me questions, so she could understand what I was going through. She never wanted me to feel inferior or inadequate. And now, she was gone. I felt entirely alone.

The clearest and most painful memory was performing her last rites and watching her body go up in flames. I had been to cremations before, but I always kept my distance and remained in the back. I felt a sense of anxiety overcome my body as they closed the coffin for the last time. I screamed, and as I held on, refusing to let go, memories flashed before my eyes: I remembered her, her voice, our greatest moments together.

Family members surrounded me, forcing me to let go, pulling me off of her. I only yelled more, kicking, refusing to leave my sister behind. Unwillingly, I followed the procession beside my mother and sisters into the crematorium. They placed her coffin inside, and as per tradition, her eldest son—only six years old—pushed the button, igniting the fire. I saw the tears in his eyes and his confusion. He couldn't understand what had happened to his mother. I was still confused too.

After a few seconds, the lid rose, and we saw the flames. She was gone. My sister had become ashes, and I felt a hole in my heart that I knew could never be filled. All I could do was scream. Life as I knew it was over.

Three months passed, and I counted each day and week without her. Things did not "get better" like people said they would, and my sister's absence did not get "easier with time." Each day, I woke up feeling worse. I went to therapy, where I cried and vented. I kept myself busy with schoolwork, but eventually, the semester ended. I returned home for the summer. There were moments I felt like I was improving. But then there were the times in a room full of people, I still felt so alone.

I was left with my own thoughts—the racing thoughts, the thoughts that judged me, the ones that questioned my goals, my values, and my future. That's my problem. Most of the time, I'm battling my own mind. Along with the depression, I found myself more paranoid. Fast asleep, I would suddenly wake up, thinking I'd heard something. The voices in my head seemed to become more and more real, and I didn't know how to function. I had never felt so lost and confused. I knew I was at the point where at any moment I was going to break. And on that random July day, I did.

I wish that was the end of my relationship with suicidality and that there was a happy ending to my story. But the truth is I will battle suicidal ideations for the rest of my life and have accepted that, one day, I will either win or lose. It's morbid, but it's my reality. There are still many days that I wake up wishing I hadn't. There are still days I pray that God would just take my life. I would be lying if I said that I didn't still fantasize about the numerous ways to end it all or make lists in my journal. There are days I hope I win the war, but there are times where the fight for my life is just so hard that it does not seem worth it.

For me, I have grown accustomed to my morbid thoughts about death. In my own way, I am fighting for my life and a will to live. Accepting my suicidal ideations has been a huge part in my recovery and my stability. My ideations do not make me weak or inferior—they simply make me a human battling her inner thoughts.

ENOUGH

BY NUPUR CHAUDHURY

I WALKED THROUGH THE DOORS OF THE POTTERY STUDIO AND TOOK A DEEP SIGH OF RELIEF. I changed out of my work clothes and into my studio sweats, turned off my phone, and pulled my long reddish-black hair out of my face. I selected my wheel for the night, laid down my tools, and got to work. I pulled out large chunks of clay from the communal pot and kneaded the air bubbles out of them, shaping them slowly into small, dense balls. I wiped down my station and brought the clay over to my wheel, where I began the gentle process of attaching it. When it was fully fused, I started to gently manipulate it from a ball to a cylinder and, with the curve of my hand, into a bowl.

I lubricated the clay with water and gently sponged it as I lifted up my head to focus on our instructor, who was in the midst of explaining pottery techniques from other cultures. One stuck out in particular—Kintsugi, the Japanese art of fixing broken pottery with powdered gold, giving it the appearance of metallic veins. This style of art highlights every fracture and break, rather than hiding them.

As he explained further, I thought of my own body and what it

155

would mean for bodies like mine—bodies that are considered broken—to be revered like Japanese pottery.

My mind wandered to a story that my mother often told me—my birth story. As a practicing OB-GYN, she demanded that a mirror be installed on the ceiling of the operating room so she could direct her own delivery. The doctors pulled me out of her womb under her clear instruction and quickly found that my hips were completely dislocated. It was so severe that I spent my first year of life in a body cast.

In my parents' eyes, I was born broken. Our first interaction spurred my mother into a constant state of hypervigilance over my body. Fixing me became her, and soon my father's, lifelong task.

It was clear that my physique was their biggest disappointment in more ways than one. Growing up, my Gujarati mother was considered conventionally beautiful—light-skinned, hazel-eyed, and skinny with hair down to her waist. She was the complete opposite of me—dark-skinned, muddy-eyed, with thin hair and a face like a roshgula from my father's Bengali side.

Dinner was the only time that all four of us—my parents, brother, and I—were together. My mother and father questioned my every move at the table. Whenever I picked up the spoon to add more rice or chicken curry to my plate, they would double-check my motive.

"Are you sure you're still hungry?" my mother often questioned.

I could feel the negative energy of disappointment radiating from them.

The situation was further complicated by my parents' professions—they were both doctors. Their medical expertise allowed them to justify being overly critical about my body.

When I was twelve, my mother told me that even when I smiled, the corners of my mouth turned downward.

"It's like you're frowning when you're smiling," she said, with her head cocked to the side, brow furrowed, lips tight.

I tried to rectify this, spending hours in the bathroom on weekends, trying to move muscles that did not exist to create a smile that I had never seen.

~&~

Meanwhile, my father's critiques raised a different set of issues.

"At the rate you're gaining weight," he would casually say, "You'll get diabetes and high blood pressure by the time you're thirty."

My parents never bothered to mention that diabetes ran rampant on my father's side of the family or that high blood pressure was a trait on my mother's side—to them, any negative diagnoses would be of my own doing.

~&~

In high school, I thought that my liberation from my parents' overprotective, over-critical gaze lied in my ability to go to college out of state. I thought that living on my own meant that I would be able to live my life the way I wanted. Without criticism. Without the look of disappointment in my parents' eyes.

I was sorely mistaken.

I had convinced my parents to send me to a college six hours away, where their daily criticism was instantly replaced. For the first time, since elementary school, I had men in my classes. At parties, I noticed them sizing me up and then promptly ignoring me to dance with my friends instead. It became clear that my body was not one that was wanted or considered desirable anywhere.

I thought that perhaps I hadn't gone far enough, so I moved even further away. During my junior year, I chose to study abroad in London and lived among a slew of South Asians. While I never did get that boyfriend that I always dreamed about, I did feel wanted for the first time in my life. Men talked to me at parties. They finally asked *me* to dance.

When I returned to the U.S. the following summer, my mother took one look at my body and ordered a round of blood tests. She said that my weight had ballooned that semester abroad. I had been so happy with my new life I hadn't noticed.

When the blood tests came back, my mother won.

I had hypothyroidism and, upon further tests, polycystic ovaries. Both conditions made it easy to gain weight and nearly impossible to lose it. These two diagnoses gave my parents the leverage to continue to involve themselves with my body.

From then on, throughout my twenties and early thirties, my visits home always included conversations about whether my face looked thinner and suggestions that I should take our dog for a walk or, even better, a run—a task they never asked my brother to do. I didn't know how to respond, so I just shut down.

After college, I moved to India and then New York. I was always careful to maintain a physical distance from my parents for my own survival.

However, they soon found a new method to make sure their critiques were heard and started relaying their concerns about my health via phone. I was constantly interrogated about my weight and pressured to move home where they could keep me in their sights. I begged them to have any other conversation with me. *What would our relationship be like if it didn't revolve around my body? I wondered. What would we talk about? How would we spend our time together?*

While it seemed like this dynamic with my parents would always remain the same, when I turned thirty-three, three things happened over the span of three months that changed my mindset.

First, I tripped, fell, and sprained my ribs while taking a walk on a Brooklyn side street. As a result, I was immobile for six weeks. When I was finally able to move around, I was so grateful for my body that I didn't care what it looked like or what my parents thought it should look like.

Second, during my yearly physical exam, my blood tests revealed that my A1C numbers—the marker for diabetes—had shot through the roof. But my cholesterol numbers and my blood pressure were fine. After many conversations with doctors who weren't my parents, I realized that it was the stress of my job that had elevated my numbers. This de-coupled the fear of getting diabetes with what I ate—a constant concern from my overreaching parents—and made me understand the connection between my physical and emotional health.

Third, I got into a severe car accident that should have killed me. My brush with death made me examine my life—where I wanted to be and what I wanted to be doing. I switched to a less demanding job that I could leave at 5 p.m. I took up hobbies, like yoga and pottery, that I used to tell myself I didn't have time for, and I started treating them as sacred spaces in my weekly schedule.

When I was thirty-five, my mother finally and surprisingly relinquished her grip on my body.

"We need to see an endocrinologist because I see that you have done all that you can do, and you have not lost any weight. And I don't know that to do."

When she said this to me, I felt like I had been set free from the cage I had been confined in my whole life, and I was floating in midair, free but entirely unsure about what I should do with my freedom.

To this day, I do not know what compelled her to completely shift her way of thinking. Part of me thinks that she just gave up.

I found joy in my mother's moment of hopelessness. My body was finally and truly *mine*. I always felt like I wanted to skin myself alive, peel back the layers, and let my soul step out. But I am finally starting to see my body and soul in conversation with one another. I'm not really sure what the conversation is about yet. We're still just making small talk.

I take a deep breath and return my focus to my bowl on the ever-spinning wheel. I am grateful for this moment in my week when no matter what my relationship with my body is, I have deep gratitude for my physical being—from one foot being planted firmly on the ground, to the other foot coaxing the speed of the wheel, to my core holding strong, to my back flexing based on the movement, to my hands guiding the clay. I am deeply grateful for all the parts of my body working together to develop a vision.

I don't know if my parents will ever adopt this idea of Kintsugi. After all, I am still obese, and my metabolism is still slower than molasses. I don't know if they can celebrate my cracks and fractures, my breaks, and irregularities. But I can.

And one day, that will be enough.

The following story contains sensitive material that may be triggering for trauma survivors and those who suffer from mental health conditions. Suicide, suicidal ideation, and addiction are some of the topics mentioned in this author's moment.

If you feel triggered, please know there are resources to support you.

U.S. National Suicide Hotline
1-800-273-8255

THE DAY I WOKE UP

BY JESSIE BRAR

I COULD FEEL THAT I was awake, but I couldn't open my eyes. Everything felt heavy. As my senses started coming together, I could hear whispers and chatter in between an incessant beep. I started to feel pain all over my body. My throat burned. I slowly willed my eyes to open. My vision blurred from the blinding light above me. As my eyes adjusted, I looked down at the hospital gown and the IV tubes running from my arm to the bag hanging above.

"How did I get here?" I quietly whispered to myself before my eyes gave way and slowly drifted back into unconsciousness.

I turned off my alarm as soon as it started ringing. I'd been lying in bed, awake for hours. Another night of no sleep. Another night of spiraling thoughts. Another night of wondering when this would end.

I got out of bed and got ready to head to campus. It was automatic at this point: Get out of bed. Shower. Get dressed. Go downstairs. Run into one of the roommates. Slap on a smile. Talk about the night's plan.

"What time do you want to go to the party tonight?" my roommate asked.

"I'm done with class at six, so I'm down for whenever. Are we going to pre here or just take shots when we get there?" I replied.

"I just have vodka, so shots it is."

"Okay, I have class, so I'll text you when I'm heading home."

"Are you going to eat something?"

"No, I'm late. I'll just eat on campus."

"Okay, make sure you eat."

"Oh my god, chill. I will."

"Okay, I'm just saying, I don't want you to end up wasted by 10 p.m."

"I'll be fine. I'll text you later."

Every Friday. Same conversation.

I grabbed my bag and walked out the door. It took every ounce of motivation to walk to campus. I just wanted to turn around and go back to bed, but I promised myself that I had to end the week on a good note. Ever since I started school, I'd have the same thought as I walked toward campus. I just need to get through today.

I always struggled more than everyone else, but ever since I moved away from home, getting through the day was getting harder and harder. All I wanted to do was sleep, but at night, I'd stare at my ceiling with a million thoughts running through my head. I was exhausted and irritated. I didn't want to talk to anyone. I had completely lost my appetite. Sometimes, I would go days without eating, but I would be so stressed with school that I wouldn't even notice. My grades were dropping. I was cutting my friends off. I wasn't me anymore.

These thoughts kept spiraling through my head, and by the time I looked up, I was already on campus. *Do I even want to go to class?* I thought to myself. *No. I really don't. Whatever. I'll go to the next one.*

I turned toward the student center and took a seat on the

couches above the auditorium. Suddenly, it began to fill up. *Ugh. There must be a presentation happening.* I looked for the exit, but I noticed everyone was already seated. *I would make too much of a commotion if I got up to leave now.*

So, I popped in my headphones and tried to drown out the noise, but the microphone and speakers were too loud. I saw two brown guys setting up, doing a cheesy warm-up game with the audience. I'd never seen them before, which was shocking since there were probably a total of one hundred brown kids on this campus of 20,000. I really thought I knew them all.

"Hi everyone! My name is Ajay," one of them said into the microphone. "I'm in my second year, and I'm here to talk about mental health. I think what a lot of people forget is that we all have it. One in five Canadians struggle with mental illness, but we all have mental health.

"When I started in my first year, I was so excited about university life, but that excitement slowly turned to terror. After the first few weeks died down, the parties ended and everyone went to class. Everyone else seemed to be getting the hang of it, and I felt like I was being left behind. It took a toll. I could never find the motivation to go to class. I felt like everyone but me knew what was going on. The only time I felt comfortable was when I was drunk at a party. That was when I didn't have to worry about anything and I could let loose. It started out as every weekend, then it became a few days a week, and suddenly I was going out all the time.

"Eventually, reality hit, and my first set of grades came in. I was failing. I was so far behind and there seemed to be no way to catch up. That was one of my lowest days. I remember feeling like this would never get better. There was no hope. That night, I tried to take my own life."

As he shared his story, my heart sank into my stomach. I knew those feelings all too well.

～❧

A few weeks ago, I found myself at the lake in the middle of the night. Staring into the dark black water under the moonlight thinking, *I could just go. I could just slip away and disappear. No one would notice.* The thought itself scared me. I quickly got up and ran home. I never told anyone.

～❧

"I knew that something was wrong. This wasn't okay," Ajay continued. "I did the only thing I knew at the time. I got an appointment with a therapist. Let me tell you, it was terrifying. I didn't want to go at all. In the beginning, I hated it, but slowly I noticed it started to make a difference. My therapist told me about how I could get accommodations for school to help me catch up and as time went on, things began to improve little by little. And now, here I am! I'm here, standing in front of you today, telling you that everyone struggles sometimes, but it can get better."

My phone started to vibrate in my hand. It was 3 p.m. I promised myself I would go to at least one class today.

Even after I left, I couldn't stop thinking about that guy. I had never seen anyone talk about mental health like that, *especially* not a brown guy. *Do his parents know he is doing this?* I wondered. *What would they think? What did the therapist say to him?*

The sound of the other students slamming their books closed snapped me out of my daze. Another class I wasted in my thoughts. I could never focus.

I walked home. No one was there yet. I was exhausted again. I sent a quick message to my roommates: Hey, taking a nap, wake me up when we want to start getting ready.

"Jessie, get up! It's like 10 p.m. We were supposed to leave by now," my roommate yelled, her voice jerking awake.

In a groggy haze, I looked at my phone. *How did I sleep through three calls and fourteen texts?*

"Shoot, I'm so sorry. Give me like twenty minutes. I'll get ready," I yelled back.

I dove into my closet and found a cute top to go with my jeans. I straightened my hair, threw on some makeup, and ran downstairs.

"Shots?" I asked, hoping to lighten the mood.

"Jessie, we're late. Let's just go."

"Oh my god, two seconds," I shouted back.

I took two shots of tequila, and we left. We started walking to our friends' house together, talking about the day and how happy we were that it was finally the weekend again.

"Did you eat?" my roommate asked.

"Yes, Mom. Can you calm down?" I rolled my eyes.

I lied. I didn't eat. I forgot again. *How do I keep forgetting to eat?*

You could hear the music from the end of the street. I loved living in a university town. You could party loud, and no one ever complained.

We walked up to the house. There were people everywhere—some we knew, most we didn't. We went to the kitchen to go mix our drinks and talk to our friends who had gotten there before us.

There were a group of guys hanging out by the fridge who kept looking out our way. I shot a quick smile over my shoulder and went back to talking to the girls. Suddenly, there was a hand on my back.

"Can I get you a drink?"

"No, thanks. I'm good."

"How about a shot? Come on, take a shot with me."

"I don't even know you," I laughed.

"So get to know me! Come on, one shot."

"It better be a good one."

We took a shot, and I went back to my conversation. He kept coming over to me, but now I was starting to feel tipsy from the three shots I took in the last hour on an empty stomach.

Why do I always do this? I should stop. I'm going to stop. After this drink in my hand, I'm done for the night.

"Jessie, we're going to get some air. She doesn't feel well," my roommate said as she pointed to our friend. "We'll be back in five minutes. Are you good to stay here or do you want to come?"

I put my drink on the counter.

"Yeah, it's okay. Go. I'll be here."

After they left, I suddenly felt my heart pounding. *Are they mad at me? Am I too drunk? Am I being annoying?*

I turned to grab my drink from a sea of red solo cups that all looked the same. *I'm pretty sure this is mine.* I drank it fast.

I woke up again. *How did I get here?*

From my hospital bed, I saw a nurse walking by. I tried sitting up, and when she saw me struggle, she came in.

"Sweetie, lie back down. It's still going to take a while to get out of your system."

"How did I get here?" I said out loud. "I don't remember anything."

"Your friends brought you in around eleven o'clock last night. They found you unconscious. It looks like someone put something in your drink. You should be okay in a few hours, and then you can go home."

Everything went numb.

The next few hours were a blur. I stared at the ceiling, wondering what happened. They discharged me, and my roommate came to take me home. I couldn't bring myself to speak.

"We went out for literally ten minutes to catch some air because she was feeling anxious, and when we came back in, you were gone. Then one of the girls from your class said you went upstairs with some guy, and I knew that wasn't something you would do. We found you on the floor. You were limp. I swear you didn't even drink that much. I don't know what happened."

I still couldn't speak. I walked into the house and went to my room and closed the door. *I know better than to leave my drink alone. So why did I do that?*

My mind went back to the black water. *I could disappear.* I left my drink alone and then picked it up without thought because I didn't care. I didn't care about what happened. Not just that night, but every night. I just didn't care, and I was losing the energy to fight it. I wasn't okay. This wasn't normal. Tears started rolling down my cheek. I don't want to die.

I thought back to Ajay's speech from earlier. He looked like me. Had the same skin. He struggled like me. He almost died, but there he was. Living. Doing better.

If he could do it, maybe I could too. I just needed to try. I needed help.

I dialed the number on the campus website. My stomach dropped as the line started to ring. I took a deep breath and reassured myself that this was what I needed to do.

"Counseling services. How can I help you?" a voice said on the other end.

"Um, I don't really know. I guess, uh, I want to set up an appointment."

THE UNFORGIVING SUN

BY PRIYAL SAKHUJA

IT FELT LIKE EVERY BUS RIDE HOME FROM HIGH SCHOOL. I slid into a bright blue seat and started gossiping about that day's drama with my two best friends. I was laughing at my friend's story, but I couldn't help focusing on how brightly the sun was shining. I could feel the sunlight highlighting every flaw and blemish on my face. *Why didn't I sit with my back facing the sunlight? Could my friends see the new breakouts on my cheeks that I had fretted about all morning before school?* Perhaps if I moved a bit over to the right, I would be cast in the shadows of the moving bus. As I tuned back into the conversation, I started to feel more than just the sunlight on my face.

I reluctantly turned my head to meet the gaze of a woman staring at me from a few seats away. She was unrelenting, almost as if she was trying to speak to me with her eyes. Suddenly, she got up from her seat. *Please get off the bus*, I thought. Her steps approached closer, and I could feel my heart skipping as she neared. Part of me knew what was about to come.

"Sorry to interrupt. I noticed that your skin has a lot of acne, but I know what could help you," she said nonchalantly. "You should try scrubbing coffee beans on your face."

The woman launched into what could have been a TED talk about the magical benefits of coffee beans. It lasted a few minutes, but it felt like an eternity. I forced a small smile on my face when she announced that her stop had finally arrived. I was mortified. I was fifteen, a member of the debate team and Model UN, a science research student, and a young girl who dreamed of becoming a doctor. But at that moment, I felt like I couldn't escape this face that people could not see past. I quickly laughed it off with my friends, and we went back to talking about the geometry class drama.

I got off the bus and burst into tears on my walk home. I cried in my bedroom for what felt like hours. This was not the first time I cried about the way I looked and felt. It was not the first time that I feigned appreciation for unsolicited advice. But it was the first time I was hearing it from a complete stranger and in front of my closest friends.

My acne consisted of painful, cystic breakouts that occupied most of my cheeks. They were so red and so numerous that it became difficult to discern what my natural skin color was. My acne felt like an uneven, uninviting mountain range on my face. Family members, friends, and acquaintances always shared their comments and suggestions, even though I never asked for any advice.

"What have you done to your face?"

"You should stop eating chocolate. That makes the acne disappear."

"My friend's daughter put toothpaste on her face, and that stopped her acne."

Most of the time, I nodded along, my face turning red, until I would finally end the conversation by politely acquiescing.

"Thanks, I'll try that," I would say.

But when yet another well-wisher suggested I should put period blood on my face as the cure to my acne, I found myself speechless, staring into space, waiting for this painful conversation to end.

Sometimes, these suggestions were directed solely to my mother.

"Why does she have so much acne on her face?" relatives would unabashedly ask her.

"You know, it's the age. I had a lot of acne at her age too. She'll grow out of it," my mother would reply with a tight smile.

As someone who had experienced this herself, she was no stranger to the commentary from others, but as a concerned mother, she would bring up her own suggestions of how to help. However, the last thing I wanted to hear was constant comments from my mother about how I looked, which led to a lot of arguments that ended with me storming off.

"Leave it alone," I'd yell.

Eventually, these looks of concern registered as looks of disgust in my head. I felt as if people couldn't bear the sight of me, and soon, I couldn't even look at myself in the mirror because I was afraid to see my true reflection.

Then my periods became increasingly less frequent, heavier, and more painful. It became a vicious cycle of hoping my period would come on time but also resenting it for being so agonizing when it did. I started to develop a very unattractive beard that I constantly waxed, which made me feel less feminine.

Every time my mother brought me to the doctor with these issues, they convinced us to treat the symptoms instead of trying to uncover the underlying causes of what I was experiencing.

I tried every single dermatological acne cream on the market, hopeful each time that this would be the ultimate cure. I spent hours reading online reviews about my new treatment, running to tell my mother that people found improvements in their skin in just a few months. But much to my disappointment, these creams did little to improve my skin condition. I would cry as I scrutinized the dry, flaky skin that emerged on top of the persistent acne. When the creams didn't work, I was prescribed numerous antibiotics, but they did nothing except kill the essential bacteria in my stomach. I would angrily throw out each squished, depleted tube of acne cream, along with empty pill bottles, feeling betrayed by all the online reviews I wasted my time reading.

I started college feeling as if I was the only one still dealing with unforgiving acne and stubborn facial hair. I wanted answers, but my body only left me with more questions.

During the summer of my junior year, I was studying for the MCAT. It was a stressful time in my life, and I didn't feel like myself. I was tired all the time, I felt irritable because of the weight I had gained, and I realized that I had not had my period in almost five months. I attributed most of my discomfort to studying and stress, but the thought that it might be something more dragged me to my primary care physician.

"Are you sure your scale is calibrated correctly?" I asked as I stared in disbelief. The medical assistant assured me that it was, but I still couldn't believe I had gained nearly thirty-five pounds since my last visit just six months prior.

"So it seems like everything is mostly okay, except your blood sugar is a little high, and your cholesterol is somewhat high too," my primary care physician said as he entered thc room with my blood report in his hands.

"But isn't it odd that I gained so much weight in such a short period of time? And I haven't had my period in a while too," I said, wanting to know more.

"See, what's important is to eat a lot of greens and to get away from all that unhealthy college food. I ate greens, and I started to lose all the weight I had gained over time. You have to eat healthily," he said flippantly.

I tried to explain that, although I could definitely make healthier choices, my eating habits didn't explain the weight gain. I was a twenty-year-old prediabetic, my cholesterol was high, and my sudden weight gain was concerning. He didn't want to listen.

I flipped through the pages of my MCAT book when I got home that day, not registering any of the words on the page. All I could hear in my head was the doctor telling me to "eat more greens."

Ugh, why was he so dismissive? Or maybe I'm just overthinking this. Maybe this is good? I mean, I can definitely eat more greens. And he said everything else is mostly okay, I thought, trying to reason with myself. *But I'm thirty-five pounds heavier. How did I manage to do that to myself?*

I fought back tears as I stared at my review book. Unable to concentrate, I turned to the internet for solutions, but the worldwide web can be a scary place when searching for a medical diagnosis. I found pages and pages of results for possible conditions, but I couldn't find anything definitive. I realized the only way I would get real answers was by seeing a specialist.

My mom and I found an endocrinologist, and a few weeks later, I had my first appointment.

"Based on your test results and your history, I believe you have polycystic ovary syndrome. Have you ever heard of it?" the doctor asked me.

All of the information that I had learned started clouding my brain. I quickly tried to remember all the symptoms of PCOS I had read about online: irregular menstrual cycles, hair growth in unwanted areas, acne, weight gain, fatigue, infertility, increased risk for Type 2 diabetes and endometrial cancer, depression, and anxiety.

I was swimming in information, but I felt like I still knew so little. I could hear the clock ticking in the background. My heart thrummed in my chest. I looked over and a mixture of confusion and concern spread across my mother's face. I heard the fear in her voice as she finally broke the silence.

"PCOS?" she asked. "I don't understand. I had acne, too, but I didn't have this PCOS. Why does my daughter?"

"I understand how overwhelming this can all be, and I'm here to answer all your questions," the endocrinologist replied.

I finally had an explanation for the myriad of symptoms that had plagued me during my formative years. And, for the first time, I had someone who wanted to give me answers to the questions flooding my brain: Do I need medications? Will I have diabetes? Can I have children? Should I have been diagnosed earlier? Why wasn't I diagnosed earlier? Will I ever be PCOS-free? What do I do now?

After some time, I became over-saturated with all the information one could possibly need on PCOS. I received information from my doctor, from my lab results, from my parents, and, of course, from Google.

This information overload made me constantly wonder whether

I was doing enough for myself. *Am I going to the gym enough? Am I eating too many carbs? Will this new birth control medication counteract my weight loss efforts? How much weight should I be losing? Am I doing this right?* It seemed as if the questions would never stop. But I had to learn to live with my diagnosis, and after so many years of facing an uphill battle to even get to this point, I was just relieved to have a name to label my body's dysfunction.

But sometimes, my anxiety about my health is still overwhelming. The scars on my face will always remind me of my struggles. I have gained back some of the weight that I had originally lost since my diagnosis. And, as I get older, the word infertility weighs on me more than it did when I was diagnosed at twenty. I can't help but feel that I am taking two steps backward for every step I take forward.

What has changed is how I react. When I feel upset about the way I look, I give myself the space to be okay with those emotions. When I fret about my weight and how tight my jeans fit on my body, I remind myself that I am trying my best to stay as healthy and active as possible. When I feel angst about the breakouts that still pop up every now and then, I rejoice in the fact that I can finally appreciate my true skin color after so many years of being unable to see it.

Now, as I walk onto the crowded bus and slide into one of the empty, bright blue chairs, I can feel the warmth of the sunlight on my skin. My hands and arms glisten underneath the bright, beaming light. I catch a quick glance from my seatmate, who analyzes my deep scars that are highlighted by the sometimes-unforgiving sun. I quickly turn my head away but stop myself from looking down at the dust on the floor. I stare straight ahead, taking in each ray of sunlight with the moving bus.

A TALE OF TWO: A (CANCER) JOURNEY BETWEEN BEST FRIENDS

BY KIMBERLY PAREKH & ANANTHA SUDHAKAR

Kimberly, February 2015

DRIPPING WET FROM THE SHOWER, I wrapped a towel around me. For the first time, I noticed a marble-sized lump on the side of my breast.

I immediately thought of Anantha. *Is it the same as hers?* I remembered back to my best friend's breast cancer diagnosis years ago and started to panic. The pit in my stomach felt as hard as the lump itself.

"Anantha, I have something to tell you," I confessed.

She was in San Francisco, and I was in Washington, D.C., but I felt so close to her. Since undergrad, we've studied together, lived together, and visited each other. Our years of friendship are based on a deep understanding and sharing of common values, but we also easily collapse into giggles over the everyday. Plus, she's been through this before.

"Kimmy, I know it will be tough, but you can do this," she reassured me. "I know you. And, remember, cancer is treatable and, many times, can also be curable. Especially if you catch it early."

I waited for the results of my CT scan and then received the call that would change my life forever.

"Has anyone spoken to you?" my doctor asked.

"No," I replied quickly.

"I'm sorry, but the cancer has spread to your spine, which means it's now metastatic," she said sympathetically. I told my parents, and we were silent. I felt paralyzed by shock.

Over the next few days, I could barely breathe, let alone sleep. I called my insurance company and consulted with other doctors for a second opinion. When I shared the news, friends and family absorbed, then reacted—but the next thing I knew, I was comforting them, instead of them comforting me.

"It's okay," I'd say.

But Anantha instantly got it.

"Kimmy, I'm here every step of the way," she reassured me.

I asked her if it was okay for me to lean on her. After all, Stage IV is the worst nightmare for women having gone through early-stage cancer. But she said she could keep distance and understood how our experiences are different. I was so grateful. Only 5 percent of women under forty are diagnosed with Stage IV cancer. It was hard to find my place in support groups filled with seniors or early stage patients whose experiences felt so different from mine.

Three months later, Anantha told me she couldn't make it to D.C. as planned.

"I have some stomach pain that won't go away, so they want to do some follow-up tests," she explained.

She called me back a few days later.

"Kimmy, they found something in my liver."

Anantha, May 2015

The phone rang as I prepped lecture notes for my afternoon Asian-American literature class. There were only a few weeks left in the semester, and I was eager for the laid-back, unstructured days of summer. When I picked up the phone, my doctor's voice sounded weary.

"I'm so sorry," she said. "I got the results from your scan, and it looks like your breast cancer has recurred and spread to your liver."

"So that means I'm metastatic?" I asked, feeling a dull shock. I gazed out of my office window at the fog spreading across San Francisco State's campus.

"Yes, I'm afraid so," she confirmed.

"Thank you, doctor. Thank you. Thank you," I replied, dazed, not knowing what else to say.

The disbelief I felt during that phone call soon gave way to anger. The timing of my diagnosis seemed especially unjust because my life had just settled into a hopeful stability. Only months earlier, I was declared cured after being in remission for five years, following a Stage I diagnosis in grad school. And, after I struggled to finish my dissertation, I had landed a tenure-track job in San Francisco, where I taught a sharp, hard-working group of undergrads whom I adored. My fiancé, Ramesh, and I had just gotten engaged in January and planned to adopt a child to grow our family.

Now, I sat shaking in my oncologist's office, pulling my oversized gown tightly around me.

"You'll have to take life two to three months at a time, between scans," my oncologist cautioned. I slumped my shoulders. I felt cheated, like an outstretched hand holding happiness and possibility had suddenly pulled away.

At first, I couldn't bear to tell anyone the news. I asked Ramesh to call my parents, whose tearful voices I couldn't bear to hear. But I called Kimberly myself. We sighed, absorbing the reality that we now shared the same improbable diagnosis.

"I'll help you," she said. "The metastatic world is so different from early-stage cancer, and I've been dealing with it for months now."

While I tried to keep a positive attitude with my close friends and parents, I vented, unedited, with Kimmy. Huddled in bed, clutching a throw pillow to my chest, I shared my frustrations: the evasive answers I received about why my cancer recurred in the first place; bitterness at the surgical fellows who casually chatted about bar recommendations while slicing open my chest to insert a portacath; the throbbing pain of keeping my fingers submerged in ice water during infusions to stave off nerve damage. We laughed whenever I revealed the latest indignity of my surreal side effects.

"Oh my god, Anantha, I'm so sorry," Kimmy empathized. "Our lives, I swear."

These weekly, sometimes daily, calls reminded me of how Kimberly and I relied on each other nearly twenty years before. After college, she moved to Japan to teach English, and I headed cross-country to start an M.A. program at the University of Washington. Although we were excited about these new adventures, we also felt isolated and lonely—other close friends settled in the northeast and regaled us with stories of weekend visits and nights out together.

So, long before *Felicity* made it popular, Kimmy and I recorded letters on cassette tapes, sharing what we were feeling and experiencing in our new homes and sending them around the world to each other. Opening my mailbox to see an envelope with Kimmy's looped handwriting always made me smile. No matter how low the ceiling in my cheap, overheated basement studio hung overhead, I could hear my best friend's voice. And it would instantly make me feel less alone.

Now, that intuitive understanding and ability to speak the shared language of existential grief felt nothing short of lifesaving.

Kimberly, May-August 2015

Thirty-eight wasn't supposed to be like this. I'd spent years addressing poverty around the world, starting schools for children in Afghanistan and India. I had loving parents and fulfilling friendships. Boyfriends came and went, but all were beautiful parts of my being. I'd been an aspiring yogi for more than a decade and a recent vegan convert. I was told by almost everyone that I was the healthiest person they knew.

In many ways, I suppose I always thought I had a good life. Working with acute poverty, I knew how lucky I was. But by conventional standards, I defied South Asian gravity. In the eyes of my community, I was expected to be married with kids, living in a big suburban house. But I always enjoyed living in my own authentic way, even though that came with a fair share of guilt for not making those who actually cared about norms happy.

But now, nothing was normative. It was hard. I mean, really, really, really hard. I lay in a hospital bed with acute burns to my esophagus due to radiation—the worst my doctors said they had ever seen. I weighed ninety pounds, was on drip morphine, and struggled to meet my caloric goals of 500 a day. My mom tirelessly showed up every day with watery mung soup, soft khichdi, and Ayurvedic potions for strength. I know she wished I could return to my old ways, even if they were atypical for a desi woman.

After I started to physically bounce back, I struggled with both the life-changing and mundane.

"I'm pregnant," more than one friend told me.

"I'm so happy for you," I would say.

I truly was happy, but the complexities for me were equally present—especially having spent my entire career supporting the education of children.

Another called to tell me her fridge broke.

"Can you believe I have to spend a thousand dollars on a fridge?"

I was silent at first and then feigned support. Everyone's problems were understandable. Meanwhile, my problem was just living. My body broke, and it's never going to get better, no matter how much money I spent.

Living with disease as a South Asian only compounded matters. *Why is it so difficult for people to talk about this?* Most of the time, there was silence, and other moments were filled with inane awkwardness.

"You know, Kimberly. So-and-so uncle had cancer, and he died. I almost had a cancer scare and thought I was going to die. Thank god, I didn't," an auntie said.

"Yes," I replied to comfort her.

At a pool party, an acquaintance from the local Indian-American community exclaimed: "It's great you're doing okay, even though you're terminal."

I stared at her and choked back tears. *I'm terminal? But I feel so alive.*

I shared these comments with my dad, who has been my saving grace for all the dumb things Indian people say. While it's difficult for some to react with empathy and understanding about disease, his deep religious understanding and lifelong disability always yielded extraordinary insight.

"Kimberly, we're all terminal, and we're all going to die. And it's okay," he said, softly with a chuckle.

Coming from him, I was strangely comforted and reminded that my Jain faith was paramount. For me, there was no better way to understand my state of existence. The notion that my state of being, including my body, was only a temporary part of my absolute existence. My body was a part of me but not all of me. I began embracing the unknown, though not giving up, and living even more present than ever. I also became more understanding and readily extended grace onto others. The silver linings of living with disease began to peer through.

Anantha, October 2016-March 2017

Understanding and grace. I eventually got there, but it was a process.

A year and a half after my diagnosis, constant changes in my treatment forced Ramesh and me to postpone our wedding. Dejected and drained, I unfollowed friends on Facebook who posted photos of joyful ceremonies and receptions.

Following a particularly grueling chemo treatment, I received the happy news that my sister-in-law had safely given birth. Thrilled for her, and simultaneously unable to hold myself together, I collapsed into tears. I felt more aware than ever that life continued to unfold and evolve as my own mortality inched closer. Motherhood, like the other possibilities held open to me earlier that year, started to fade away.

Seeking respite, I signed up for Commonweal, a cancer retreat in the quirky seaside town of Bolinas, California. I spent days in grief therapy alongside women from my Bay Area metastatic support group. We listened to each other's stories about the endless adjustment to nausea, fatigue, GI upset, pain, paralysis, depression, and immune suppression that accompanies cancer treatment. We shared our struggles balancing marriage, parenting, dating—life in all its facets— amidst chronic illness, and I realized my journey was not unique.

Every young cancer patient is, as author Kate Bowler puts it, "stumbling in the debris of dreams they thought they were entitled to."[1] The disappointment I felt about my own losses gave way to compassion and admiration for the gutsy, hilarious, and determined women who are brave enough to share their deepest fears and tentative hope with me.

One afternoon during a free hour, I walked to the cliff's edge next to our retreat center. The ground sloped toward a thin beach where waves crashed with calming regularity. I looked out at the glassy expanse of sea, breathed in the salty air, and felt gratitude for the ways I had been able to nurture others through my role as a daughter, aunt, friend, and teacher. The small victories of surviving each day and feeling loved left me content and at peace.

---

[1] Bowler, Kate. *Everything Happens For a Reason, and Other Lies I've Loved.* New York, Random House, 2018, p. 121.

The following year, Ramesh and I finally got married in my hometown of Austin, Texas. To my surprise, my close relatives all flew in from India to attend. I was unsure what they might think of a forty-year-old bride, let alone one with cancer. I anticipated bristling against their quiet shame. But as I walked toward the mandap, escorted by my uncle, as is South Indian tradition, he winked and grinned at me. I grinned right back, uplifted by the unconditional love my family had shown me.

After the ceremony, Kimmy helped me change into my lehenga and plucked grains of turmeric-stained rice from my hair. Later, we crowded together on a hotel ballroom dance floor and laughed with my cousins, flinging up our hands with uncontainable joy.

Thanks to a new clinical trial, my cancer treatment started to stabilize, and life readjusted to a sometimes-disrupted form of normal. Ramesh and I honeymooned in Paris and Venice. I published enough research to earn tenure. And Kimmy and I visited Mexico City with our best friends, traveling together for the first time since our diagnosis. We felt back to ourselves again—more grounded, revised versions of ourselves.

Kimberly, May 2019

The new normal had set in. I let go and accepted my disease. But I had not given up. I did everything in my power to stay and be well. I was holistic in my approach, keeping up with a vegan and gluten-free diet, daily yoga practice, and weekly acupuncture.

Years into my diagnosis, I was thrilled when the disease finally became stable. The scans were spaced more widely apart—from three to six and, eventually, nine months. I obsessed and monitored the reduction of measurable cancer cells through an Excel sheet. I came back into my life with a vengeance.

I was consulting full-time at the World Bank and UNICEF on education, my first love. I continued living and thriving, from trekking a glacier in Patagonia with a close friend to swimming with hammerhead sharks with my sister and nephew in the Galapagos to hiking with gorillas in Rwanda. My heart was full again. And, others with cancer were being referred to me to learn about complementary health approaches.

I started writing about my experience and had my first speaking engagement at a Komen conference. After four and a half years, cancer had become more of a narrative than a disruption. Anantha and I continued to be each other's support. Our journeys are so similar, yet distinct—just like us.

But then I heard the news again.

I put the phone down, numb. My cancer had progressed. I was a unicorn no more. I didn't even know what to do with myself, so I watched an episode of *The Great British Baking Show*. Not so bad, those Brits. I felt like they were competing for themselves, not each other. *Me, too,* I thought. *I'm competing with myself.* I felt like I was starting all over again and I hated it.

I picked up the phone and called Anantha. She, too, was going through a treatment transition. We were able to relate, more so than ever. I had a lot on my side: an arsenal of health care providers who I trusted, acute knowledge about my disease, a team of family and friends, and, lastly, my own sense of being informed by faith. In theory, I knew I would be okay, but all I wanted to do was hug my friend.

Anantha, June 2019

Over time, my clinical trial medication began to fail, and my cancer grew and spread to my bones. It was close to my birthday when I learned that my cancer had progressed, and the irony of celebrating another year of surviving metastatic cancer while feeling the ground slip from under me once again was not lost on me.

As a gift, Kimmy surprised me with news that she had nominated us for a yoga and horseback riding retreat for women with breast cancer. We'd been talking about attending a retreat together for years. And so we met that summer in Big Sky, Montana, feeling totally out of our element and loving it. We groomed dust-caked horses and heaved ourselves into stiff leather saddles, riding unaided along a river trail lined with aspen trees.

On the last night of our retreat, we collapsed into Adirondack chairs that faced a small pond on the ranch grounds. My hands burned from a new chemo treatment that blistered my palms. I cooled them against my glass of rosé.

"Not bad for two girls who haven't been on a horse since Girl Scouts," I joked, as Kimmy laughed.

"Seriously!" Her voice softened. "I'm really glad we got to do this together, Anantha."

"I know," I replied. "It was so special to have so much time here, just the two of us."

We dropped into a comfortable silence, watching the sun slip from the sky.

KIMBERLY & ANANTHA, EPILOGUE

More than five years into our diagnosis, we have come to see our experience with cancer as an evolving journey of adaptation and development. If figuring out how to live with cancer has taught us anything, it is this core truth: it is possible to appreciate the beauty of life, one that is entirely meaningful and happy, but challenging all the same. This realization has only deepened our bond. We know our friendship transcends disease, yet now fundamentally includes it. We continue to lean on each other, moving forward.

relationships

The following story contains sensitive material that may be triggering for trauma survivors and those who suffer from mental health conditions. Suicidal ideation is a topic mentioned in this author's moment.

If you feel triggered, please know there are resources to support you.

U.S. National Suicide Hotline
1-800-273-8255

THE GOOD GUY

BY RAJVIR GILL

TWO DAYS AFTER I FOUND OUT MY HUSBAND CHEATED ON ME, he called to let me know that he was bringing his mom to couples' therapy.

"You're kidding, right?"

I tried to keep my composure as I drove to our appointment, but all I wanted to do was rip out my steering wheel and leave what happened next to fate.

"Look, she just wants to make sure I am okay. She will sit in the waiting room. She's just scared of what you'll do to me. She wants to support me," he said.

This grated at me. Why was this all about protecting him? For the past two days, his parents had been protecting him from my rage, my parents had been telling me not to yell, and my friends had tried to make me stay away from him because I was too angry. I feel like they have all muzzled me. *Screw this*, I thought, gripping the steering wheel.

"Are you a child, or are you a grown man? If you cannot understand why that is inappropriate, I don't know what to say. Drop her off at a Starbucks and pick her up after. Jesus."

She was the last thing I needed. She was the woman who once sat across from me, all motherly with her soft exterior, suit, hair in a proper braid and dollar store slippers, telling her son that if he wanted someone to cook for him, he shouldn't have chosen *this*, with an outstretched hand in my direction. The last thing I wanted was for her to see me and remind me to be a sayarni kuri.

"Okay, okay. I'll talk to her," he said.

"Thank you."

There were red flags from the start. And I saw them. I knew I would never grow to love the city he had chosen for us. I knew he would never want to pick up his life and live in another country to help me pursue my career. I knew that I couldn't meet his parents' expectations of a good Indian wife, and I knew he was liable to shut down when I needed him the most. But he was a nice man, a good man—the tall, professional, Canadian-born Punjabi man that all Punjabi immigrant parents dream of for their daughters. He was still the person who said he would never understand my pain but that I would never find another man who would be more willing to try to understand than him. His smell became my signal that I was home in the right arms, with my head nestled perfectly under his chin. He is still the man who was so kind, gentle, and honest, whom I would spend years with even when I knew I was beginning to disappear.

And, probably most importantly, he saw me as this wondrous, unique creature after I had spent years without feeling seen and understood. Having previously lived in Europe on and off for the five years before I met him, it was nice to not be a fetish for European men and to be seen as more than the weird brown girl who doesn't belong anywhere. After so many years of feeling like an afterthought, I saw the red flags as things I needed to change about me in order for his version of love to be enough.

And of course, it wasn't.

Now, we are sitting across from our therapist as I speed talk, recounting all the details: how he told me about his infidelity at 4 a.m. when he was drunk and his parents were visiting; how his parents hovered over me as I cried, telling me his cheating was my fault; how I knew the woman; how he turned to his mistress and confided in her about my illness and our relationship. I dump the contents of the betrayal on the floor and hope that it will finally begin to make sense. Our therapist sits there patiently through my version of events, but I notice she keeps glancing at him. We sit on opposite sides of a too-soft leather couch, and as I speak, I look over and see him staring straight ahead, tears falling, with a panicked look in his eyes.

Fuck how he's doing. Stop looking at him. This isn't about him. I have a right to be angry.

After I am done venting, she finally breaks her gaze from him and asks what I want.

"I want someone who has my back, that will support me, that I can trust. I know I am not unlovable. I know I have a lot to give and I want someone who sees that," I say.

"Yes, and there may be someone out there who can be that for you, but on the other hand, you might not find such a good guy again," she says, smiling sympathetically.

As soon as the words come out of her mouth, I want to punch them both square in the face, but knowing full well I don't know how to punch and with a quick vision of me being arrested for said punches, I let her continue.

"Yes, he did a bad thing, but that does not mean he is a bad guy. If you want to move on from this, you have to leave the past in the past, no questions about the affairs, move forward, start fresh, and make something better."

Here it is again. It's about protecting him. It's about letting go of my anger. It's about him being a good guy. I have heard this the whole time we have been together—how lucky I am to have such a good guy. If cheating and neglecting your wife doesn't make you a bad guy, then what does?

To add to that, it's only been forty-eight hours since I found out, and I am already being told that it's time to move on. Years before this session, I checked myself into the hospital and sat in a room that could double for a locked prison cell—barren, one bed, an ominous-looking door with the obligatory monitoring window, and one of those personal DVD players from the early 2000s meant to distract me from the fact that I was there because I wanted to die. When my husband finally arrived, he looked around the room, exasperated, pulled up a chair, leaned over, and asked:

"Why are you doing this?" He was desperate, at a loss, searching for something to snap me out of it. "You know, walking down here I saw a man with an amputated leg—you should be grateful."

And when he said this, I was transported back to when I was growing up, crying on the kitchen floor with a mother telling me that I wasn't depressed, that I was lazy. So, when the attending doctor eventually came to see me, I lied.

"I'm okay," I said.

What did I have to be upset about? Yes, I had a shitty time, for a long time, but technically at that moment I was in the clear, everything on paper was good. I was married to a good man, I had studied, traveled, and lived all over, I had two degrees, I had been able to work in a field that I was passionate about, and I was finally, finally, in law school. So why now, when everything was so good? But the thing with surviving a history of depression, family violence, death, and emotional abuse, is that it finally gets you when you're out of fight and flight mode. It gets you when you have it the most together because you've let your defenses down.

If there was a silver lining to that visit, it was being referred to a program that provided a thorough assessment from a team of mental health professionals. But when my husband came home from work that day and I rushed to tell him their findings, all he said was:

"You're seeing professionals, what do you need me for?"

He didn't say this with any callousness. It's actually what he believed was best for me, ignoring the fact that I wanted and needed him to walk through this alongside me. When I sent him articles to better understand my conditions, he never read them. He didn't have the time, he said. He's too tired from work, he said. So my days went on. Each day, I tried to focus on school, but I had this heaviness and fog in my brain that wouldn't go away. I wanted to get out of bed and apply myself, but I was so tired that waking up and forcing myself to be productive felt almost violent. The only way I could save myself was to take a medical leave from school.

To my friends from law school, I was a liability; to my friends outside of law school, my pain was too much or I wasn't as ingrained in their circles as I thought I was. So for the next four months, my days and nights consisted of rotting alone in our bed, without seeing or speaking to anyone for days at a time, counting the hours down until my husband came home so I would have someone to talk to.

Every day, as I lay there, convincing myself that David from Schitt's Creek and I were meant to be best friends and patting myself on the back for solving the crimes of Law and Order: SVU before the reveal, I couldn't believe all I had fought through in my life had led me to this.

I finally had time to fully realize the extent to which my husband had failed me. All of my grievances throughout our marriage resurfaced: I blew up at the fact that I gave up the wedding of my dreams for the big fat Indian wedding his parents wanted, I brought up all the times his parents were aggressive toward me—because I didn't speak Punjabi, because I wanted to go back to school when I should be making babies, because I was sick when I should have been taking care of my husband, because I didn't dance or watch Indian movies, because I was taking their son away from them—and he did nothing to defend me. I raged about him always choosing work over me the very few times I asked him to stay home when my depression was at its worst, and I blamed him for boxing me into a life full of the cultural rules that, as a child, I had promised myself I would leave behind as an adult. Ignoring me made me rage to get his attention, and my rage gave him a reason to continue to ignore me.

"I think what you both need is to figure out what you want."

Our therapist's words pull me back to reality.

"I want you guys to go home this weekend and work on a vision board. Figure out what you each want and how to do it together. Putting it out there will help you see a way to get there," she continues.

I want to roll my eyes, but I don't. Right now, my vision board looks like a blur of knives, tears, and broken hearts, with the words "How dare you?" scrawled across the top.

Still, I agree to go home and make these vision boards because, right now, I will do anything to distract myself from the decision I know I have to make. But we never get to our vision boards because when we spend the evening with our magazines, poster boards, scissors, and glue, I discover there was yet another woman. I don't let knowing the details go, and I'm not easy on him. The more I uncover, the more I realize he has never had my back—that when he cheated, he was punishing me for being ill, and most cruelly, that while I was sitting at home alone, he was getting support from these women. *What about my support? What about supporting each other?*

In the next session, the therapist urges me to move forward. To understand that my illness made him depressed, which had a part in his infidelity. Again, I find myself thinking, *It's only been three weeks since I found out, and I'm already supposed to forgive. What Twilight Zone hell is this?*

These sessions make me feel hopeless. I have been to enough therapy to know that the therapist is filtering every word I say though my diagnosis. When you have mental health labels, everyone assumes that your default state is the extreme of your illness. When I'm talking about my relationship, all she sees is an out-of-control, self-destructive, abusive person. But because I work on myself, I know I have never been those things. Yet here she is, mentally checking off the DSM-V symptoms as I speak because I am the broken one, and broken people break others.

I'll admit she gives him some rules too. He has to stop turning to his female friends for emotional support, put a pause on traveling for work, and establish boundaries with his parents.

But less than a month after our last session, he tells me that he is going out of town for work and is taking his female co-worker. No consultation, no consideration for how I feel. When I begin to tell him why I don't want him to go, he blames me for interfering with his work. So I give in, but I can feel the resentment creeping in again—choking me, making me smaller.

He comes back from this trip with stories about his course. I smile weakly. If I am not happy for him, I am a horrible unsupportive bitch in his eyes, and if I am happy for him, I am not admitting that he disregarded my bottom line by going in the first place.

"That's great. I am happy you enjoyed the course."

As the words leave my mouth, I know I am defeated.

He then goes off to take a shower, and I see his phone lying on the couch. Half of me doesn't care anymore, but the other half wants to know how stupid he really is. I pick it up, heart beating, and I open his messages looking for texts from anyone with a vagina.

As I scroll down one thread, there is nothing sexual, but he is still using a woman as an emotional crutch—this time about his guilt about cheating, and she is confiding in him about her past relationships. Once again, he is turning to another woman instead of me. It's only a matter of time. Another drunken night. Another day I am the ugly, depressed version of myself. Another fight where he storms out of the house in the middle of the night. I don't scream, I don't throw the phone, I don't cry. Instead, I know what I have to do. I can't police this man for my whole life. This man has a problem. And he's convinced himself that his problem is me.

When he comes out all fresh, clean, and relaxed, I tell him I'm leaving. He's once again exasperated and tells me that he didn't do anything wrong, and that I am the one not doing my part by refusing to use any of the strategies from therapy. He says he can't talk to me right now because I am too angry. He's right. I'm pissed. I don't want to do the fucking strategies. I don't want to turn toward him, and he obviously doesn't want to turn to me. I have to get out of here.

I have been acting my whole life. As a child, I had to act to make sure the people around me were happy amid the chaos. In adolescence, I had to act as though what was happening at home wasn't the start of never feeling safe. And in my twenties, I had to act to make sure I was liked. And finally, my best performance—that I could forgive him and continue to live his life.

I move out. Months later, I find myself driving to my new home after another day of classes of talking to myself in my head, exchanging pleasantries and trying to shut down the urge to stand up in class and start screaming. As I drive, I half listen to my podcast, half think about what he did. I park. Every moment is a conscious effort now. I go to the elevator. I meekly smile and say hello to the person already in the elevator. I fumble with my keys, press the button to my floor. I exit the elevator, get to my door. I grab my key. But now I stop my autopilot and lean my head against the door. I can't believe I am here again. I can't believe I am alone. I want a person to accompany me through life. I want the career, the independence, and the best friend. I imagine trying to meet someone. How will I ever trust again? How will I meet people? Dating apps? They didn't exist when I met him. Aren't all the good ones paired off by now? I am thirty-five. I feel my eggs dying with every turn of the clock. God, I've already been rejected by my husband, and I don't need strangers to join in on the fun too. Feeling vulnerable, I call him.

He answers.

"I didn't want this to end. This wasn't my choice. I didn't want to be with another person, I can't believe I'm here again. I can't believe I have to start over," I mumbled into the phone.

He doesn't see it that way.

"What do you mean? You are not at the same place you were. You have finished your third degree, which will open so many doors for you. You've lived and traveled in even more places, and you're now free to go after what you always wanted. I'm really excited for you. I'm excited to see what you'll do next."

And this advice, this encouragement he is giving me, is what makes leaving so hard. Because he is not evil. Within him, there is still that best friend that thinks he's my biggest supporter. But maybe he is evil—hurting someone so deeply, who was already traumatized to begin with, giving me a masterclass on deceit. That's not a best friend—that's worse than an enemy. So this is why his words don't land the way he thinks they will. I'm glad that he's excited for me. I'm glad he feels ripping my heart out is the push I needed to follow my dreams.

But nothing excites me about this new future. It's hard to be excited when you're too exhausted to even think about getting that job you always wanted and moving to a new place, knowing that there will be no one at home waiting for you. It's hard to be excited when you don't know what was real in your marriage and what wasn't, and it's hard to be excited when you keep learning that you are disposable. Maybe he was right, and there are only good things ahead.

But right now, I continue to fight the urge to sleep all day. I continue to remind myself that I should not binge drink wine on a Tuesday. I continue to convince myself that McDonald's is not a cure-all. I continue to challenge myself when I want to shut others out for not being what I need when I don't even ask for help to begin with, and I continue to try to be kind to myself.

But every time I close my eyes and try to sleep, I see us. I see us on our first road trip—when our relationship was still a secret to our parents, and it felt like the world was behind us and the future belonged to us as we were driving. And I was in the passenger seat, excited, hopeful, and riding a high that only the beginning of a love story can give you. I turned my head to look at his profile and saw the face that had once made my stomach flip. He took my hand and raised it to his lips with his eyes still locked on the road ahead. And I felt his soft lips on my knuckles and his handsome face against my hand. I wanted to be there forever, us moving in the same direction toward endless possibilities.

Then I open my eyes, and all I see is the blank ceiling. All that I see now is a blank slate I wasn't prepared for. I'm scared. More frightened than ever. I'm suffering. I'm in despair.

But I know that as lonely as I feel now, I was alone in that marriage. That is why I'm certain that whatever is at the end of this tunnel, it's not going to be settling for a good guy. It's going to be realizing and really believing that my survival wasn't all for the reward of being rescued by a white knight. It was about finally knowing that I'm worthy and building a life that is worthy of me.

It's time to stop staring at blank ceilings. It's time to get out of bed.

So I sit up, throw my legs over the edge, brace my hands on both sides of me, press down into the mattress, take a deep breath, and rise.

PUTTAR

BY NISHA SINGH

WHEN MY DAD PASSED AWAY SUDDENLY IN JANUARY
2015, my mom, sister, and I knew that he would have wanted us to
fulfill all the appropriate rites and rituals according to Sikh tradition. I
mean, the dude always listened to Kirtan CDs in his car. Unfortunately,
we had no idea what those specific customs were or how to go about
doing them. So, I did what millennials do best, and googled the shit
out of it. I still came up mostly blank as it seemed that these details
were passed down patrilineally and not via the interwebs. We leaned
on some of my dad's friends and family for these details but quickly
discovered that funeral customs in South Asian culture don't give
much pride or place for women or daughters, and so, for the most
part, we weren't needed.

Under any other circumstances, I would have immediately balked at
the blatant misogyny that was slowly unveiling itself in these traditions.
But I already felt myself ceding ground, and the guilt that I didn't have the
cultural knowledge to understand how last rites even worked chipped
away at me. In order to give him the funeral I thought he would have
most wanted, I very uncharacteristically kept my mouth shut.

The week after he passed, his funeral proceeded in a blur around me. Even though I anticipated feeling a massive void without my dad around, I didn't imagine how quickly I would begin to feel an artificial distance between us, as others seemed to have a more intimate knowledge than I did of what was truly important to him.

After his paath and funeral, it was clear that there was no custom or tradition that would give me a place in my dad's final rites and farewells unless I pushed for it. So, I negotiated for a responsibility that, frankly, I didn't really want. I asked to take the ashes back home with me to Washington, D.C. This was partly because my Gujarati-Hindu mother was feeling superstitious about keeping ashes around their house while I—in the words of *The Office's* Michael Scott—was only "a little stitious" about it.

In my mother's defense, it is both Sikh and Hindu custom to scatter ashes as soon as possible after someone passes away, and thus Indians more so than Americans seem to get the jeebies if they keep loved ones' ashes around for too long. When my sister, Priya, and I decided that I would bring my father's ashes home, we also made the choice to scatter them at Haridwar, where his own parents' ashes had been spread.

Our family ridiculed us for delaying the final ritual of our father's last rites.

"This is selfish. Not scattering his ashes right away will prevent your dad from attaining the ultimate peace," one relative said.

Week after week, I was criticized and told that I should have someone else disperse the ashes on our family's behalf if I couldn't put my father ahead of my own needs. But, given our long financial and legal to-do list after the funeral, we had no choice but to delay the trip. So every week, I choked down my own doubts and pushed back against the pressure—for my sister's sake and for my own.

It was difficult to explain back then why it was so important to me that my sister and I be the ones to scatter our dad's ashes. I knew abstractly that we had been robbed of the chance to spoil him in old age and we would never be able to repay him for the strain and sweat he expended to build a life for us here in America. So, even though these new ceremonies didn't hold a personal meaning for me, I felt that it would be the last chance for us to do something that was truly for him.

Over the next ten months, I was driven by this nebulous but potent desire and my very stereotypical eldest child Type-A tendencies to navigate the only to-do list I've ever hated. I regularly commuted back and forth between my life in D.C. and my mom and sister's home in Texas, where I tried to support them while also planning an ash-scattering getaway to India for two.

Ironically, the more I immersed myself in planning the trip, the more distance I felt growing between my dad, myself, and my Punjabi-Sikh identity. I continued to avoid what I knew would be a complex grieving process by working through a tangible and simpler to-do list that conveniently drained me of any remaining energy. This was a foolproof strategy—until it wasn't.

Eventually, I wound up in an urgent care center feeling like I would choke on my own saliva. I was diagnosed with ulcers and was prescribed a week of bed rest. My therapist at the time asked if the doctor gave me an explanation for the sudden onset of ulcers and my generally declining health.

"Well, she said too much caffeine, citrus, tomatoes, chocolate, or smoking can cause ulcers."

My therapist raised his eyebrows.

"Did she mention stress as a potential cause?"

I looked away.

"Yeah, but I wouldn't say I have been more stressed than I usually am."

"Yeah, you're right. It's probably just excess tomatoes," he said dryly.

Making myself sick with stress, planning the ultimate last rites for my dad, and battling relatives' remarks about when his ashes should be spread all seemed to crash down on me. I realized for what felt like the first time that I would never again hear my dad's gruff but joyful voice greet me in his easy Punjabi-English banter:

"Hanji, puttar? Ke haal? Your bakwaas Astros are never going to make the playoffs again if they keep trading half their players each year."

With all the pressure I put on myself to have a stake in my dad's last rites, I never stopped and checked in with my grief.

How could I find the heart to listen to bhangra again without accepting that I would never sit on a long car ride with my dad, belting out the tunes of *Apna Sangeet* on repeat from one end of the beltway to the other? How could I learn and accept the traditions that others told me were so important to my father while knowing in my heart that nothing would have been as important to him as the fulfillment of his daughters' wishes and happiness?

I rain-checked these weighty questions and anything resembling emotion as I shepherded the flight-compliant urn containing my dad's ashes into my carry-on baggage and, even later, when I held them on my lap for the twenty-four-hour flight to India.

New Delhi traffic was infamous—so infamous that in order to avoid it on our five-hour journey to Haridwar, Priya and I willingly dragged ourselves out of bed for a 4:30 a.m. departure. The air was cool and misty, a respite from the powerful heat that would soon rise with the sun.

We greeted our driver, Mann Singh Ji, and within minutes, we hurtled northward out of the city on the empty highway. The sky was still dark, but the roads were already bright, illuminated by merchants opening their stalls.

Priya and I had been in India for less than twenty-four hours, so between the jet lag and weaving around bicycles and trucks, over potholes and bumps in the road, we were both wide awake and actively fighting nausea. I could see Mann Singh Ji glancing into the rear-view mirror at us occasionally. He was confused, I suspected, by the two clearly related but suspiciously silent young women, separated by a backpack strapped between them with a seatbelt.

With a Gujarati mother and a Punjabi father, the only Hindi I have in my language arsenal comes from Bollywood movies. That being said, I also hate making people speak broken English just so I don't have to speak broken Hindi, Punjabi, or Gujarati—and this feeling is infinitely compounded when traveling around India. So, when Mann Singh Ji finally broke the silence and asked what brought us to India, I quickly realized that my linguistic studies—reading the English subtitles while watching Bollywood movies in Hindi—had not remotely prepared me with the appropriate vocabulary for this situation.

"Woh...uhhh...hamare Papa ki asthiyan...Ganga mein," I said, while awkwardly miming pouring something into the air with my hands.

He quickly picked up on what I was not able to say and let me trail off.

"Akele?" he replied sympathetically, glancing from me to my sister in the rear-view mirror.

I glanced up and could sense Mann Singh Ji's nervousness at the thought of dropping us off on a riverbank to fend for ourselves. But I nodded and smiled to reassure him—and myself.

"Aap dono bahut ache kaam kar rahe ho," he said, nodding back at me.

I patted the backpack which held the urn containing my father's ashes and smiled again. I wanted to believe him, but I was a little less assured.

After some more broken conversation, Mann Singh Ji called his eldest brother to find out where exactly he had scattered their own parents' ashes and then insisted on driving us there directly so he could help us buy supplies and find a priest.

Haridwar is considered a holy city—hundreds of thousands of Indian nationals and international tourists alike travel there each year, so I was surprised to find the riverbank and market lanes relatively quiet. Granted, thanks to our early departure, it was still only 10 a.m. when we pulled into an unmarked lot near the river. As we carefully navigated the winding, cobbled dirt roads in the general direction of the riverbank, we turned a corner and entered an expanse of stalls and tables selling the offerings, leaves, and flowers we would need for the ceremony.

Mann Singh Ji asked if we had any specific preferences for the last rites. I glanced at Priya for her opinion, but her eyes had glazed over, her expression showing a mixture of anxiety and anticipatory sadness. I shrugged back at Mann Singh Ji and hoped I was sufficiently conveying that all the carnations looked equally carnation-y and acceptable to me. We stopped at a nameless stall to purchase an armload of flowers and prasad before we continued toward the riverbank. As we approached flat steps leading into the water, I knew we had arrived and it was finally time.

A priest approached us as soon as we reached the river's edge and—having no real basis for comparing priests or services—we promptly accepted his offer and gave the requisite donation. We sat on the last step, closest to the water, to begin the ceremony. Here, the river was calm, and it was narrow enough for me to make out details of the people sitting on the opposite bank in front of the pastel pink and white stucco buildings. The sun was bright overhead by this point, and I could smell agarbatti in the air, a pleasant substitute for the scent of dust that sat heavy in the afternoon heat.

Priya and I listened as the priest recited prayers in Sanskrit. The flow of words registered as a calm buzz against the still morning air and only faltered when he gestured to us to do our part—throw a bit of water over here, put your hands there, tear up flowers to offer into the river aise hi. Finally, he gestured to us to bring the urn forward and scoop the ashes into the river together. At first, we only offered a bit at a time while the priest continued to chant, and then we overturned the urn and poured out the ashes until not a single grain remained. We watched as they commingled with the other offerings in the river and floated away. Some of the prasad sunk quickly to the bottom while the flowers floated past our line of vision to join the river's onward current.

After a ten-minute ceremony, a five-hour drive, a twenty-four-hour flight, and ten months of planning, we had completed the final ritual in a long and painful goodbye to our dad. After the priest walked away, I couldn't read Priya's face, but her silence worried me.

"We don't have to leave yet. Do you want to walk around and stretch our legs a bit?"

Her shoulders rose and fell in a weak shrug.

"Sure."

We wandered the riverbank aimlessly while Mann Singh Ji hung back to give us some space. We took a photo of the exact spot for posterity and surrendered our remaining ceremonial offerings to some thankful monkeys. On a nearby footbridge, we looked over the river that would supposedly carry our dad's ashes back to Punjab—a place he had never lived but where his soul would reunite with his parents' and find peace. We lingered there for a while, staring out at the picturesque scene. Priya half-turned to me, her face still unreadable.

"I guess I didn't think it would be over so fast," she said.

A lump grew in my throat. I nodded back, not trusting my voice. I knew what she meant. The actual ceremony felt anticlimactic for such a significant goodbye. Or maybe she was referring to the fact that Pops was only fifty years old when he passed away, leaving us in our early twenties with the broken promises of years he was supposed to spend with us. At that moment, still fighting off the tangled web of grief I would come to know in the months that lay ahead, all I could think about was our ten-month struggle to assert our right to say the final goodbye to our father.

Back on the banks of the Ganga river, and in the shared silence with my younger sister, I felt the cracks around my carefully contained grief start to spread. Without the comforts of a to-do list to guide me or a cultural legacy of sexism to rail against, my insides writhed against my growing sadness and wondered as I thought about Priya's words again while we walked back to the car.

Our feet dragged with the knowledge that this painful goodbye was just one of many stops on this new journey without our dad that grief would yank us through. I looked at my younger sister, who had grown so much older—too old for a little sister by my measure—

in those ten months alone. My throat was still constricted, my gut wound too tightly into itself to allow me to reach out to her to offer or seek any comfort.

As we walked further from the river and away from the stalls, the path narrowed again, forcing us into a single-file line. Heat radiated from the early afternoon sun to replace the misty morning chill, and for the first time that year, I took a long breath to soak in the warmth and shifted to the side to let Priya pass ahead of me and lead us onward to the next stop on our journey.

A SACCHARINE SICKNESS

BY SAAHIL

I HAVE A SPECIAL TALENT for hiding in beds without anyone knowing I'm there. It must be my thin, petite stature that makes my body blend in with the natural folds of the blankets and comforters. I also have short breaths, so my body doesn't do the usual expanding rise-drop-rise-drop that other heavy-breath bodies seem to do. And I rarely snore.

So I basically sleep like an angel.

Strangely, I also sleep with a pillow on top of my head. Please don't ask me why because I don't have a proper answer. I don't know if other angels also do this, but I'm open to being the first. The definition of an angel needs to become more expansive, and I certainly welcome the opportunity to pioneer more inclusive angelicness.

You see, I grew up on shows like 48 *Hour Mystery*, so I have an escape plan for every hypothetical scenario. I like to think that if my house were ever broken into by some murderous sociopath, I would make it out alive. I do have a special ability for hiding myself under covers, after all. Maybe I would be able to call 911 in secrecy. But I don't know if the officers who show up would really want to help us.

A few months ago, the police arrived at my house at 3:41 a.m. Ignoring our very visible doorbell, they abruptly started banging on the front door right next to my bedroom. My first thought was that they were random people in fake uniforms who were going to rob us. My second thought was they were white supremacists out to kill us.

These uniformed men were loud and sounded angry. I wasn't planning to let them in until I heard my mom passing through the hallway about to open the door by herself. Her measured footsteps sounded courageous.

I don't know what made me think I would be able to defend my mom against the aggressive men outside of our door, but I went to fulfill the ambiguous duty of protecting her. We cracked the door an inch and peeked through the gap. I asked to see their badges and asked what the problem was. They said they wanted to speak to my brother.

My brother is on the autism spectrum. The emotion he most exudes is anger. He feels the universe owes him something for having wronged him by giving him a condition that society does not accommodate. He holds a lot of resentment toward both the people in his life and complete strangers. His anger is justified, but it's also debilitating to his growth.

Our ableist society gave advantages to me and my sister while marginalizing my brother. Sometimes he has been the center of the joke, and other times, he's been erased completely.

I'm guilty of this erasure too. Most of my friends learn I have a sister at the beginning of our friendship but find out I have a brother much later. In some of my short-lived friendships, they never realize I have more than one sibling.

The police cared little for this backstory. The policeman of East

Asian origin came in to speak to my mother and me, while the three white policemen took my brother outside. My brother wasn't wearing a shirt on this chilly winter night, so my mom went to retrieve him a jacket. We were all trembling.

My mom and I found out the police had come because my brother had made a threatening post online that was flagged by the government. The police showed up to make sure he wasn't a danger to himself, us, or anyone else in society.

"I know my son, and this is not like him," my mom said, concerned. She continued to insist that this action was not representative of his kind heart. Although her face was flushed, her words had backbone.

Throughout this entire ordeal, my dad somehow remained in his room—on the opposite side of the house from my mom's room. He was either sleeping very deeply or felt profoundly indifferent—perhaps a combination of both.

Convinced he was awake, I stomped to his room.

"You might want to wake up, and if you're already awake, you might want to come to the living room," I said. I wasn't sure how accurately my sarcastic tone could be interpreted so early in the morning. "The police are here."

This behavior is exactly the type of passive-when-convenient, aggressive-when-convenient behavior that has made my mom sick of my dad over the past thirty years of marriage.

"Coward," she calls him. "Heartless," she calls him. "Selfish," she calls him.

Over the years, as I grew into my own person—much to my Indian mother's dismay—she started using the same insulting words toward me. The cliché offenses felt like knives when coming from the person who used to be my refuge in this family. As emotions escalated, words became weapons.

Two months before this incident with the police, my mom emailed me and my dad:

```
I'm looking for a place to move to. Dad will also have
to sign the contract. Will keep you posted.
```

My dad claimed it was his first time hearing about it. This is exactly the type of passive-when-convenient, aggressive-when-convenient behavior that has made my dad sick of my mom over the past thirty years of marriage.

"I want a divorce, and I'm taking the kids to Miami" was the mantra I grew up hearing during the daily fighting. "The kids" was the collective, monolithic entity that was always cited as the reason my parents stayed together. We were the reason behind this war, the kindling to this flame—something we never asked for.

I don't know the minimum threshold of activation energy that my mom finally experienced to inspire her to send this email. I haven't lived her life—I'm merely a product of it, historically a mediator in the middle of this complex marriage's crossfire.

Growing up, I witnessed my mom hating the anniversary gifts my dad got for her every December 15. After a particularly disappointing year, she mandated his inclusion of a gift receipt. The last gift that he gave her was a crockpot, which they ridiculously and silently fought over by hiding it in various kitchen cabinets. This crockpot was the first gift they both seemed to want, and separation from each other seemed to be the second. And so, on their next anniversary, she gifted them both by signing the lease to a new home.

At first, I assumed she was excited to move in without wasting any time. However, she spent an excessive amount of time decorating her former house, wanting to leave it ornate before her permanent departure.

January passed. I started going to therapy.

February passed. The police questioned my brother.

March arrived. My mom was still in the house.

That spring, she asked my opinion on what vases she should leave perched on the shelves. I continually expressed my apathy, resenting her for caring about something I thought was trivial.

I regretted having temporarily returned to a house I no longer considered home. My intention was to help them cleanly separate by moving heavy boxes and pacifying any tender emotions.

When April came, she was partially moved out, but I still found her sitting in her former room in a house she no longer resided in. The door was locked. I later questioned her about it, and she jokingly asserted it was her "ex-room," providing no other details.

I immediately laughed to buy time, not knowing what to say.

"See, I make you laugh! I always make you laugh," she taunted me with her motherly charm.

"Mom, this is unhealthy," I said finally.

Soon after, I found her in the kitchen—her ex-kitchen?—drinking wine.

"Didn't you hear how rudely he spoke to me?" she asked me after I heard them fighting over a dusty-ass ottoman. To be clear, this ottoman must have been worth ten dollars max and didn't even have a future being restored. Yet, they went back and forth about it, arguing, volumes escalating—a sound reminiscent of my childhood. There was apparently confusion over who purchased it and when. Ultimately, my mother claimed victory and continued to complain as she carried it out the door, out of the house. Dad was fuming as if taking the ottoman was a personal attack.

That was the price of peace in our household: $9.99.

"All I can do is drink," she said as she sat in the kitchen, self-medicating with low-quality white wine. I partook, pulling out an identical mini bottle from the fridge, drinking half of it with her and the other half in my room by myself.

May arrived, and she was still in the house. Instead of packing up pieces of artwork on the walls, my mom went shopping to replace them. During this period of several months, she continued to fix nightly dinners for my dad—rice, roti, two sabjhis, and a small salad—served to him on a tray as he watched TV in his room.

I repeatedly question this act, always hoping for a different answer, as if repeatedly opening the same fridge door hoping new food appears. She poignantly regards this as her daily duty. She says it makes her a good wife. I am shocked to hear her voice tinged with pride associated with an act I classify as submissive. But what do I know?

On certain days, I found my mom quietly eating kichadi in the kitchen with her hands. She usually employed normative eating politics and ate with a spoon, but on those days that I quietly entered an even quieter kitchen, she would keep her eyes down. These were the days I knew she needed to talk the most and cry the most, depending on whether words or tears fell out first. Sometimes tears conveyed more.

I believe in these moments, downcast gaze and eating with her hands, she was recreating a physical gesture that transported her back to Bombay—the land of the rasas, flavors you can savor with your hand.

Ayurveda deconstructs the tongue's palette. Meals are intended to reflect the balance of these six rasas: sweet, sour, salt, bitter, pungent, and astringent.

The sweet dish is dispersed throughout the meal and nibbled in between bites, rather than isolated at the very end. Since the rasas represent the natural elements—space, air, fire, water, earth—isolating one rasa in high concentration inevitably creates an imbalance.

It was ironic that my mother was the one to teach me this concept. I realized this wisdom describes exactly what the separation was for her—a long-awaited dessert, a saccharine sickness, confusing to consume all at once.

How does one move from non-love to un-love? Sometimes there are no answers, I learned. Sometimes things just don't make sense. My parents' marriage was heavy in bitterness, their separation heavy in sweetness—a whiplash of flavor.

By the time June came, she fully moved out. She took all the bowls but left all the spoons. My dad immediately started purchasing ready-made food from the local Indian Cash-n-Carry, completely unbothered by the change. It seems the constellation of rasas concocted by his wife was easily exchanged for that of a stranger.

In my community, tradition expects an engaged womxn to change her first, middle, and last name after she gets married, tethering her full identity to something curiously *auspicious*. Meanwhile, the husband's name goes unchanged.

My community also has a tendency to casually toss around the term failed marriage. My existence derives from a failed marriage. I wondered what one does when failure is differentially shared between one stakeholder whose social identity was rewritten and another whose remained the same.

Growing up, my mom would frequently remind me to marry a "nice, Indian, Hindu girl."

"Well isn't that what you and dad did?" I would reply.

Her laughter in response was always bittersweet.

MEETING MY FIRST BLOOD RELATIVE

BY CHANDRA COATS

I BREATHED A HUGE SIGH OF RELIEF. I had done it. At last,
I had given birth. When our daughter entered the world, my husband,
who was in shock from the delivery experience and normally suffers
from severe anxiety, gasped:

"She's...white?"

The surgeon, an Indian doctor married to an American man and
who happened to be seven months postpartum herself, stifled her
laughter. I, on the other hand, did not and chuckled openly. I couldn't
wait to see her. Our baby was here. As I recovered, my husband texted
me a picture of her in the isolette at the NICU. I saw our features in
her—she had my husband's chin, ears, and eye shape, but definitely
my nose, long eyelashes, and dark hair. There she was, my only known
blood relative.

Dan and I had always pretended with close friends and family
that we didn't want kids, but the truth was we were buried in student
debt. During that time, we also faced health issues. Conception and

pregnancy had not been easy. There were exams, ovulation test strips, a fertility app, months and months of waiting. Until finally, one pregnancy test showed the coveted symbol we'd been longing for.

"It's positive," I told Dan quietly.

It was like time stopped as we stood there holding each other, filled with joy and fear. We talked about how and when to tell our families. I called to set up my first prenatal appointment, and he requested a bit of time off work to go with me.

I parked my car near Dan's, and we walked into the doctor's office together nervously.

"I need to speak with you regarding the decision to have an anatomy scan," the doctor said in a matter-of-fact tone. "This is the mandatory disclaimer from the state. We have to warn you that it may or may not be covered by your insurance provider. It could possibly result in a very large bill."

"We'll talk about it," I said, looking over to Dan.

The idea of an anatomy scan was just as frightening as it was intriguing. I don't know my family's medical history, and getting a glimpse of it through this scan was the closest I'd come to learning more about a part of me that I'd never had access to.

"I'd like to get the scan if it's fine with you," I later told my husband.

We checked with our insurance and the scan was covered, but he couldn't make it the day of the appointment. I was uneasy because I lied to my boss about needing to go to a dentist appointment and because the medical building was in an area of San Diego I wasn't familiar with. I pulled my tiny car into the parking space with a stork on it and sat awkwardly in the waiting room with other pregnant women. The appointment didn't take long, and I thought everything went well. I saw a strong backbone and a well-formed head, but I couldn't make out much else. *What if I carried a genetic condition?* There could be unknown health issues, behavioral or otherwise. I got a call that evening to schedule another appointment.

I went in the next day. The obstetrician stepped into the room and immediately looked directly into my eyes and said:

"I wanted to explain this to you in person and not scare you over the phone. During the anatomy scan, it was confirmed that there is only one artery in the umbilical cord instead of two and there is an anterior placenta. Single umbilical artery occurs in about 1 percent of pregnancies. I would say I see about one every year. A strong correlation is when the child has predominantly Caucasian ancestry. We don't know why. It's just an observation. An anterior placenta can make it harder for you to feel the baby move because it makes a cushion. I wanted to assure you that both are rare, but they don't mean your pregnancy is considered high risk. Precautions just need to be taken. Don't go on Google."

I left, feeling uneasy about the information the doctor gave me. In my head, I kept repeating the phrase: 1 *percent of pregnancies.* But even with these new worries, an old one crept up again—I still didn't know anything about my own genes, at least nothing definitive I could grasp onto.

My mom somehow pried the information out of me during a phone call after I drove home.

"They said not to worry," I said, trying to convince her. She was also prone to anxiety. She called me back about an hour later.

"I'm sorry. I did exactly what you asked me not to do. I went on Google, and I couldn't stop crying."

I was immediately frustrated. I did not need the additional worry of trying to micromanage my mom's emotional burden. Neither of us had been pregnant before, and in a way, my pregnancy was living out something she could never experience. I had to accept that, while allowing myself opportunities to respectfully make my own space.

How would my Indian mother have reacted? I thought. During my entire pregnancy, I was caught between two major unknowns: my first mother and my daughter. Throughout my life, I could describe my first mother's presence in figurative speech. She was like a ghost in the room or a breeze that rustles leaves then disappears. It's so different from the presence of the mom I grew up with.

Everything I knew about my Indian mother was from an adoption document: "Young. Unmarried." Unfortunately, I learned from other adoptees that the wording does not vary on any of the adoption documents from that orphanage, so there is speculation as to whether or not it was accurate. Only names and dates were stamped onto the forms. In my imagination, my first mother always remained young, unmarried, and unknown. Throughout my pregnancy, the curiosity about her drifted in and out, like an old silent film shifting in and out of focus.

The weeks before my daughter was born, there were kick counts, non-stress tests, false labor, and an extra week of waiting. I remembered one particular visit with the nurse practitioner at the obstetrician, she reminded me a lot of my mom—tall and blonde.

"Have you decided on a name yet?" she asked.

"No," I laughed. "Do couples ever agree on names?"

Dan and I each had names we liked but didn't love. It was a hard decision. I wanted a name different from anyone we knew but not too unique, easy to pronounce, and not Indian. She threw her head back a little as she chuckled.

"My family's Slovak, so we were the first ones not to choose super traditional names."

"Are you serious?" I gasped. "My husband's grandmother is Slovak. That's her first language. We think we'll have her name, Rose, as the middle name," I said, feeling a little jealous.

The loneliness of that moment was sudden and strange. I had no cultural matriarch. In moments like this, my bond with my daughter grew, but I became more aware of how my connection with my Indian mother was lost forever. I longed to sit with her and ask her about the day I was born. I didn't even know my real birthday. I imagined her sitting in my home next to me, sharing her pregnancy stories over tea—or maybe chai, I guess.

My husband and I carefully went over the birth plan, and I packed a duffel bag with all the extra things we would need for the hospital stay and tucked it into the trunk of my car. We installed the car seat and checked it a few more times to make sure it was securely fastened. As my giant belly grew even larger during the last few weeks, my uncertainty grew with it. During one of my non-stress tests, the nurse rushed over to me.

"We got a picture of her face. Do you want to see her?" she asked.

I was thrilled. This was the first time I was really going to see my daughter fully. I looked at the image on the screen and laughed. I saw a slightly slouched baby with dark hair, impatient eyes, and a small scowl.

I was supposed to be induced, but the hospital didn't have a space ready for us. We waited in a triage room and looked everywhere for our carefully written birth plan. It was nowhere to be found. Despite being a week overdue, I suddenly felt unprepared. We fell asleep to the sound of monitors keeping track of our baby and me. At four in the morning, a room finally opened up. The birthing suite was large, and at sunrise, we enjoyed a gorgeous view of San Diego and the Pacific Ocean.

Somewhere on the other side of that ocean is a woman who doesn't know she's about to become a grandmother, I thought to myself. I couldn't express my need for my first mother at that time, but it was there. I certainly bonded with my daughter before she was born, and I wondered if my first mother had felt the same with me. *What did she really think as she felt me move inside of her, even as she gave birth?*

It's hard to go along with the popular adoption narrative—that my first mother relinquished her rights to me so readily and flippantly. As she carried me inside her body, she had also carried part of my daughter. There, in the hospital, I couldn't help but wonder, *Did she plan to give me away or was it a spur of the moment decision?*

She was representative of India, a synonym. I found myself missing a place I had only lived in for three months as an infant. The grief of being separated from this unfamiliar home grew inside me along with my daughter. I ached and longed for experiences I never had and never would have.

My mom, sister, and my husband's family soon arrived.

"You're so calm," my mom said as I received my epidural. She held my hand as I inhaled and exhaled slowly and deeply. She was a retired labor and delivery nurse, so I took it as a huge compliment.

My husband had taken our teenage niece to our favorite Indian restaurant, which happened to be a block away from the hospital. Her father lived across the country, and Dan checked in with her regularly to see how she was doing. I thought it was sweet that he took the time to do that, especially since a few weeks prior, I had joked with the restaurant owners:

"If you see my husband here without me, you know I'm having the baby."

Now they knew. Although I had not expressed anything beyond this, I realized it was important that he was reinforcing the multicultural aspects of our family without me present.

"I'm so sorry. I didn't mean to miss it," he apologized, panting from running to our room.

"It's okay. My mom was here," I reassured him.

In the morning, my doctor came to our room.

"I know having a C-section isn't your first choice. It wasn't mine either, but I promise that I'll do everything I can to make it as comfortable as possible for you. At this point, it's about safety. I just had the surgery myself," she said.

As I rolled into the operating room, I remember being excited and wonderfully drowsy. A few minutes later, I heard my baby's first cry. My husband stood next to me, and our eyes filled with tears.

"Mommy's here," I called to her.

"Daddy's here," he said after me.

"Okay. Her uterus is back in," the doctor said.

"Oh, good," I joked to myself.

The first day felt like forever. I woke up alone in my hospital bed. This was not on the birth plan.

Recovering from over forty hours of labor and an emergency Cesarean, my whole body hurt. It wasn't until the next day that I was able to work up the strength to visit the NICU, but I still couldn't hold her until the day after. I looked at her chubby little face and sleepy eyes. This time, there was no scowl. I was so overcome with emotion I could barely speak. She responded to my voice as soon as she heard me.

"Mommy's here," I greeted her. I sat with her in my weak arms feeling so happy. I pretended to count her fingers and toes.

"Oh, good...all eleven," I said.

My husband laughed at me. Some color returned to his face as his smile reached his eyes. I tried to take in every detail of my daughter's face. And, at least for a brief moment, the questions about the past melted away as I held the future in my arms.

HOME

BY DURIBA KHAN

A MIASMA OF SMOG, CURRY, AND TOBACCO penetrates my nostrils as I scrunch my nose in disgust at the dilapidated airport in Karachi. Humid, sticky air clings to my Aéropostale hoodie as I take in my surroundings: hugging, crying, and babbling families; battered Samsonite suitcases; and large LED signs misspelling things in English. I already miss Texas' Southern hospitality, smiling, friendly white people who say "please" and "thank you," and most importantly, elevated toilets. This Pakistan is very different from the one I grew up hearing about from my father. I think back to one time we saw lush rolling hills in a Bollywood film.

"Beautiful," he admitted. "But nothing quite like Pakistan."

"Is there any way I can go back home?" I lean over and whisper in my mother's ear. "*Any* way?" I repeat.

She grits her teeth to form a smile, lightly elbowing me in the ribs as a group of three guys—apparently my third cousins—walk over to greet us. I look over at my father's face and notice his eyes are especially sparkly tonight. A tear slips from his left eye, and my scowl softens. He stares into the polluted sky blankly, and I imagine that he's lost in thoughts of a simpler time.

While we make our way to the pickup lane, hordes of relatives swarm us and envelop us in hugs and slobbery kisses. We pile into a taxi and speed away, my sister and I uncomfortably perched on my mother's lap.

"Welcome home, brother!" my uncle calls out joyously, embracing my father. I swear I hear his bones crack, but he doesn't seem to mind. My grandma places a kiss on his temple, and tears fill her eyes when she sees my little brother, now seven, for the first time.

"Where did the time go?" she asks me, pulling me into a hug. Unsure of how to respond, I freeze. I want to miss her, but I don't. I see my sister smile politely and hug all of my relatives, much to my mother's approval, and I follow her lead.

An hour later at my cousin's house, I am greeted by an overabundance of fried foods and relatives, who possess a fascination with pinching my cheeks. As my grandma coats my mother's tresses in coconut oil and shares stories of my father's childhood mischief, I look around the room to see smiling faces. Family members—many of whom met me for the first time today—tell me they missed me.

"Pakistani mangoes are just something else," my aunt says, seconds before popping a piece of one into my mouth. She isn't wrong.

As the din of a family reunited after years continues to fill the air, I glance in my dad's direction.

Pappa originally wanted to be a singer, but his father had other plans for him. My father left Pakistan over two and a half decades ago—the first person from his small village to ever do so—to further his medical education in America. Pappa put his heart and soul into his studies and went on to become a psychiatrist in Texas.

Now back in his familial home, he has fun answering all of his family's questions about America, from "What do white and black people look like?" to "How do you get halal meat?" He seems at ease.

❧

The next morning, I am woken up by the sound of a rooster's call, coupled with my aunt's voice pestering her four-year-old son to stop climbing the roof naked. I sit up, confused as to why the benches surrounding me are unoccupied.

"The whole village is up, and of course, you've just risen!" my mother reprimands, as one of my cousins makes a bad joke about spoiled American girls.

Being in Pakistan is painful for me. Here, I am simply an American, and in America, I am simply a brown face. In America, "back home" is South Asia, and in South Asia, "back home" refers to America. *Which land is truly mine? Why do I not feel safe and at ease in either place? Where do I belong?*

In the bathroom, I try brushing my teeth using only a bucket of water. Frustrated, I call out to my mother who doesn't respond. I long for sinks and showers. I scan the villa looking for her until I spot my mother and father strolling hand-in-hand in the surrounding sugarcane fields, pointing and smiling. The Dhuhr prayer athaan sounds.

"How did you sleep?" my twelve-year-old cousin, Feriyaal, asks.

"Well, I could see the moon but could also feel ten million mosquitos trying to kill me." I stick my tongue at her jokingly.

We are hopping on rooftops when I notice a boy, maybe thirteen, watching us from below. Feriyaal looks at him shyly. I nudge her shoulder, and she admits that they are betrothed to one another. My sister and I exchange confused looks.

"You guys wouldn't understand," she says accusingly. She's right. We don't.

At night, I slap the fourth mosquito to land on my arm. I shift on the takht as the sound of crickets and men playing poker echo in the distance. I look over to see Pappa sound asleep only three benches away, beads of sweat lining his upper lip.

"Pappa?" I call out. "Once the sun comes up, it'll be impossible to sleep out here."

My mom shushes me. Pappa opens his eyes and winks at me playfully.

I want to ask him if he feels like I do. I want to ask him if he just wants to go home to Texas and use a sink to brush his teeth and sleep on a mattress. I wonder if he also feels like a stranger in a place that is supposed to feel like home. I turn to my side. How different would my life be if I was raised here? If he didn't do something I would never have the guts to do?

The year was 1991. A young man with a chiseled jaw and curly black hair stepped foot in O'Hare International Airport in Chicago. He had left everything behind, taking only his teary mother's blessings, good luck wishes from the village, and a fake Nike duffel bag.

"What is your reason for entering the United States?" a stern Border and Customs officer asked, her brow furrowed.

"Um, to stay with some friends and spend some time learning," the man murmured nervously. Normally witty, he was surprised that these were the only words he could muster. She nodded as he moved onward, each step taking him closer to his destiny.

After the young man was dropped off by a chatty taxi driver at the address he was given, he glanced around nervously before knocking on the door before him. He was greeted by seven men who, like him, had decided to try their luck at the American dream.

"Welcome, brother!" they called out, embracing him. This was the first time he had met many of them. He spread his paisley-patterned comforter on the floor of the one-bedroom apartment and went to sleep alongside three other men. But sleep did not come easy. Instead, they spent the night chatting and reminiscing about their lives back home.

"Do you remember the sound of the athaan at sunset?" someone asked.

"Oh man, I miss the street food," another called out.

The young man's heart filled with nostalgia. He wondered if he should pack his bags and return home, if he'd even make it out here. Then he reminded himself that after coming this far, he couldn't give up.

Chicago was not kind to him. He didn't have a Green Card, and he worked late nights at a clothing shop in the bitter cold of downtown. Although his good nature and lightheartedness earned him a spot in the hearts of his roommates, he wasn't so lucky with hospital residency programs right away. When he called home, he heard about the expenses and the struggles. His meals were twenty-five-cent chip bags, and his spirit was fractured. Both lasted him longer than expected.

One night, a day's hard work between hospital rotations and clothing store shifts brought only troubled slumber. He slipped out of the covers and carefully stepped over the snoring bodies of his roommates, making his way to the fire escape. He climbed the rattling ladder and sat on the highest rung, admiring the city's sparkling lights. His heart ached for home.

∿

In the morning, I wake up to the sight of Pappa in his white salwar kameez, pushing an ice cream cart and parading around the village. Ambushed by children, he walks slowly, laughing with them while handing out ice pops. My father is usually smiley anyway, but this time seems different.

It must be something about this heat or the satisfaction of his mother's homemade daal on his tongue after decades. It must be the feeling of his father's comforting hand on his shoulder or the sound of his sisters and brothers speaking Saraiki, his mother tongue—a language I never bothered to learn.

Whatever it is, it seems to be working. Because for once, after years, he seems at home.

That night, as I sit up and watch the moon to distract from the sweltering heat, I am lost in the stars twinkling over Pakistan. Now, my heart aches for home.

IN THE EYE OF
THE OWNER

BY NINA MALAGI

WHEN I ANNOUNCED MY ENGAGEMENT, none of my
friends had understood what was going through my head. Later,
they were equally confused by my divorce. Over the twenty years
of my marriage, no one put a scimitar to my throat, and this was no
BBC drama where the Asian girl is smuggled out of her West London
suburban home and married off at her parents' whims. Now, I don't
fear coercion from others so much as I fear the restraints that I
unwittingly impose upon myself.

A three-bedroom flat, situated in a well-sought neighborhood
in my ancestral city of Ahmedabad, Gujarat, was the only remaining
legality binding my husband and me together after twenty years of
marriage. Our children were grown, independent, and incurious,
never having spent even a single night there. We rented out the
apartment over the years and it made a profit. When a too-good-
to-turn-down offer came, an old familiarity allowed us to discuss
the question of selling in a matter-of-fact way over text, the way you

might talk about picking up milk from the supermarket.

Now the leaky pipes were patched, walls painted, and the marble floor polished to the point of treachery, ready for the best offer.

"We both need to be present. The buyer insists," my ex-husband wrote. "Don't flake out."

I bristled at the command.

I instantly wanted to fall back into old patterns, to pick up the phone and rant:

"Flake out? And what about you? Where the fuck were you all those years when I needed you to be present?"

"Mind your language," he would reply with his usual outdated Indian-English admonishment. He never uttered any profanity in all the years I knew him, and I would put the phone down, not knowing if I should laugh or cry.

I could recite every moment he had not been present. Don't misunderstand. It's not that I spend time ruminating bitterly on all the things that were wrong in my marriage. I just found it prudent, before seeing the man I had loved for years, to be well-armed and remind myself of the list of reasons why I left him. To pulverize any voice inside my head that might whisper, *Maybe it wasn't that bad.*

If I had to pick a color for my failed marriage, it would be the sun-faded rotten-orange curtains of the London maternity hospital where I gave birth to our first daughter. Alone.

"My husband's an engineer, working in America, so he can't be here with me and the baby," I said, needing to explain away the young-single-motherhood stigma.

My eyes met the cold stare of the ward nurses, which read as, "Yes dear, that's what they all say."

I was at my parents' home when my water broke in the afternoon. I calculated the time in New York and phoned his office extension.

"I'm heading to the hospital. Tell Dad which flight you're taking when you get one." The contractions were twinges in my lower back, like someone wringing out wet laundry.

"I cannot simply just drop everything and come. I just started this job. How can I leave?" He spoke in a level tone, not wanting to attract attention from his new co-workers.

After a thirty-eight-hour labor, the baby was so beautiful and tiny that I sat up the entire night, watching her as she slept in the crook of my elbow. My friends came to visit us with flowers and tiny clothes. Each carried their disbelief that I was by myself.

"Why isn't he here?"

"The woman *always* goes home to her parents' house to give birth and the husband turns up months later," I patiently explained. That's how we do it in Indian culture, I lied. And I shamed them for false cultural insensitivity to silence my own shame.

The large deposit for the flat was an overly generous wedding gift from my father. Two days before the wedding, I argued against the gift with the callousness of someone who always had a home provided for them.

"It's so unnecessary," I had said.

My grandmother's huge knock-off Le Corbusier bungalow, built in the fifties and exacting cement in the style of the Great Brutal was large enough to host a grand wedding.

"What do *you* think of this?" I asked my husband-to-be.

He considered every aspect with seriousness.

"It's an investment. Or think of it as our retirement home." He pulled out maps of our city, blooming into a phase of development promising a fantastic trajectory. "Besides, don't look a gift horse in the mouth. It's so nice with all the marble."

The apartment was the first of many decisions that my husband would make for us.

I don't want the flat. "But it's an investment."

I don't want to move to the U.S. "But it's such a great opportunity."

I don't want to stay married. "You're crazy."

I don't love you anymore. "Who cares? We're not teenagers."

I don't want to feel miserable all the time. "Anyone can feel anything at any time. It doesn't make it real."

My married life had been woven out of pressure, guilt, and coercion. The flat was the final piece for me to unravel.

A trip to India is not for the fainthearted. Too much baggage, really. But I am truly in love with my city. Every time I come home, my city puffs its chest out like the brave rabbit chasing off a wild dog with its barred buck teeth. The medieval invader Shah Ahmed mused about what peculiar courage must spout from the dry riverbed to make a rabbit so fierce. And my city pins medals on me—*well done for making it back*. There is a river, and while it used to trickle like the Mahatma's last geriatric piss, making a dilapidated backdrop for Henri Cartier-Bresson to capture, now it flows lustily through a city of high rises.

My ex-husband sent a chauffeured car before dawn to the sleepy airport, and I wondered if he still had his own hair, grown fat, or had become too feeble to come in person. Then I remembered we never used to do things like picking each other up.

Before crossing the stodgy Victorian iron bridge, I asked to stop at the shrine of the old fort city to see Goddess Ma Kali, the protector, standing guard in front of all crumbling gates and doors.

I had decided to stay in the flat. As I climbed to the third floor, my luggage became smeared with whitewash from the narrow walls of the stairwell. Standing in front of the polished heavy teak door, I smelled the inside before I could see it. Burnt incense, its ash straws dropping in a brass plate. The flat flinched when I dropped my baggage in the middle of the empty open marble floors. A few weather-beaten rattan chairs by the balcony remained next to a card table with torn green felt and terracotta pots of lush once-loved plants, immovable since their bases had cemented to the floor a long time ago.

"You can't stay here. It's empty," my cousin, who once upon a time was a wild dancing child at my wedding, said. She had left a trail of sequins and plucked all the marigolds from my flower garland as she sat in my lap all those years ago. No sequins today. Everyone wears jeans now.

I squeezed her hand.

"No, it's exactly what I want. I'll be okay."

She looked doubtful, this now-married woman who spoke perfect English and managed a huge household full of in-laws and small children.

The ancient fridge shuddered in the corner.

"I'm a hundred percent serious. Will you be all right here by yourself?" she asked. Her direct eye contact met the same light brown eyes. "So, when is he coming?"

"Later," I smiled. "Look, take these for the children, and I'll stop by after." I unpacked the two tins of duty-free Quality Street chocolates. "I know you like the green triangle ones."

She grinned. "Thank you. There's milk in the fridge, and call me when you are ready, I'll send the driver."

The most normal thing to do while I waited was to spend the next few hours alone preparing to see him in-person. To show him what he missed, what he lost. But even a brave rabbit has the good sense to scarper and camouflage itself from the thing that would destroy it. In my case, it was making sure my shirt hid the tattoo he would hate. I tried to finish reading my book, feeling irritated that he had real estate in my head again.

The lock of the door rattled, and I knew he was letting himself in. *You need to ring the bell*, I thought irritably. The lock was so old it took time, but I did not get up from the chair.

"Hello," he said, without a smile, and all his features arranged in order.

"Hi."

I knew we were already tired of each other, as the low light of the early evening is wearied by the heat of the day. I poured him a glass of bottled water. I did not forget my manners, but my thoughts were graceless. His hair was all gray now. He was thin, but a hint of curvature in his shoulders suggested his backbone was letting him down.

"I'll make some tea," I said.

"Okay, sure. I'll be quick about this."

We had papers to sign and the realtor's fees to discuss, and we needed to solve the mystery of who had the original deed. A new one would have to be patched together and pushed through the red tape of Indian bureaucracy.

I had the practiced ability to tune him out as he explained the remaining work to be done.

"The buyer is ready to pay more than the asking price. We should get it done as fast as possible."

I was distracted by the sounds from outside—a series of distant whistles from a pressure cooker and car horns. A ritual preparation for the inevitability of night, when all monsters grow in strength.

"You know, we could stand to make a lot of money on this. You should think about investing, don't be—" he said, cutting his words as he stood by the balcony staring down at the vehicles parked below. "You should plan better."

Oh yeah? Like we planned our own grand wedding like two premature generals, promoted to head the campaign on the sole merit of being the only ones left on the field? I wanted to say, but I didn't.

"You're frowning at me again," I stated, not looking up from the papers I was busy initialing.

His exasperated Brahminical restraint held well under the assault.

"I told you, I am not. I do not."

His nose is of a delicate South Indian design, not constructed well at the bridge to perch eyewear, unlike my northern beak, and it makes him constantly wrinkle his nose and furrow his brow. "Buy new glasses," I used to say.

"I need you to sign an affidavit for the court to declare that the flat was never a part of any dowry," he said.

And here it was—a frown and a deep interest in skimming the skin off his tea. This was the way we made each other squirm, and now it was not so prolonged in its unpleasantness since there was no bind, just enough of a reminder of what was broken.

"I can't sign." I sighed.

"What?" he exploded.

"I can't sign for something in a language I can't read," I explained. He had forgotten. I could only read numbers in Gujarati.

"If it's a local court document, it won't be in English," he relaxed. "I'll get it translated."

He is familiar with this role, being more Indian to compensate for me.

I don't want my silence to be read as acquiescence.

"I'm not selling," I said firmly.

"This is ridiculous, you came all the way out here! And now what? Is it more money?" he said agitated.

I moved to the other side of the room, closer to the front door. "I look like an idiot, everything is ready. Your dad was such a rational person. How did you turn out..." he continued.

I could finish each one of his sentences. Unstable. Broken. Thoughtless. Selfish. Useless.

There was a sharp snap of the rubber band in my head. Those were his words and I refused to subscribe to his narrative.

"Not a good idea to bring my dad into it now, don't you think?" My quiet coldness shocked him.

"Now what happens?" he repeated. Our children once observed that when their dad doesn't get what he wants, he simply repeats it, rearranging the order of words. "What happens now? We have to agree to something. What? We just keep renting it out?"

"I'll find a way to buy you out."

He shook his head, and scoffed, "With what?"

"That's not your problem." *I will figure this out*, I assured myself. "In the meantime, renting is the best option really."

"I'll leave these papers for you to look at and hope that either you are too jet-lagged to really make any decisions, or you are crazy to not see this amazing opportunity."

He left.

In our marriage, all the dramatic exits were his—except for the last one. On my own, I seethed. *What's his problem? Why is everything back to "You're the crazy one?" I can take some space to work out how* to buy it if I need it. *All the space in our marriage was always rented out; it's not like we had real joint ownership of anything.*

I phoned my cousin. "Hey, it's me. Yes, I'm ready. Do you know anyone in the bank who can help me figure out a loan?"

I rinsed the teacups under the running water. He had held this handle, I realized. I scrubbed it with more force. I set the teacups to dry and surveyed the kitchen, the dusty walls, the deadened plants. My steps reverberated as I crossed to the doorway. I imagined the apartment in the morning light, a young family struggling with boxes, their togetherness. I took one last glance and walked out into my city, letting the door slam behind me.

MOTHERLY INSTINCTS

BY ANITA WADHWANI

OH GOD, PLEASE SIT IN THE CORRECT SEAT, I thought as
my mom and I walked into the dark theater.

"We have to sit in the seat listed on the ticket," I told her, as if I
was talking to a small child.

She nodded, and I quietly breathed a sigh of relief. After fumbling
in the dark while the previews played, we managed to find seats F5
and F6.

With our feet up on the leather recliners, I intently looked at my
sixty-eight-year-old mom sitting next to me. Her smile stretched
from ear to ear as the Bollywood comedy started to play. The sight of
her with tears of laughter dripping down her face twenty minutes into
the film allowed me to relax further into my seat. Calm and happiness
washed away the anxieties of the last few days. Getting us settled into
a new routine, a new normal, has been one of the biggest challenges
of my life.

My mom is a proud, college-educated Sindhi woman exactly
thirty years older than me. She's one of the few Indian women I know
who has always preferred shorter hair, whether it be a bob or even

249

a pixie cut. Nowadays, her short, thick black hair is streaked with strands of grey, which frame her North Indian features nicely.

On good days, she looks like most women in their sixties, the kind who have an affinity for bright lipsticks and big earrings. She remains strong, physically and mentally, despite the number of challenges life has dealt her. Her health has been complicated by aggressive Type 1 diabetes, bouts of mental illness, a stroke, and now early-onset dementia. She also suffers from paralysis in her right hand, a complication from the stroke, which limits her ability to do the things she loves freely—cooking, putting on a saree, and writing letters with her impeccable penmanship.

On bad days, she's agitated and impatient. She stomps her feet and yells when she doesn't get what she wants or is confused and frustrated. To a random onlooker, she may appear to have behavioral problems, be intellectually disabled, or just seem like an angry, old woman, depending on how she lashes out. To my dismay, she's also extremely stubborn. Maybe it comes with age. My mother cannot be convinced into doing anything she isn't set on.

Being her caretaker in my thirties was never part of the plan. And I'm a big-time planner. I had envisioned where I would go to school, what jobs I would take, and where I would live to a certain degree, but I had never foreseen this. After my father's death, I had no choice but to become her guardian. Any other scenario would come at a heavy price—loss of freedom for her and an overwhelming guilt for me.

The movie credits rolled, and holding her hand, I helped my mom navigate in the dark, just as she used to do with me when I was a child. I kept her close to me and held her steady while walking to the parking lot.

"We need milk. Oh, and onions, potatoes—" she said, as we passed the grocery store.

I cringed at the thought of taking her to the store with me, but there is comfort knowing that these activities will wear her out for the day.

Taking someone with early-onset dementia to do simple errands demands a number of notable traits—patience, understanding, a good temperament, quick thinking, and a lot of energy—all of which I can say, I have in either limited or low supply. But, after years of doing this, I, too, have my good days.

In the car, I flashed back to six years ago, and I finally understood why my dad became so short-tempered and frazzled. I fondly remembered the last few weeks of his life, when he and my mom came to visit me at my new condo in Virginia. At seventy, he was a far cry from his active skier, tennis player, skinny days, but he still looked like a man who was at least ten years younger. The only sign of his real age was probably the complete loss of his thick, dark locks that he was known for back in the sixties. He and my mother were in their thirty-fourth year of marriage. Life had dealt them numerous challenges during that time, but they had gotten through all of them together.

"Things seem like they're getting worse," I said to my dad when we returned to Alexandria from a museum outing in Washington, D.C.

"This is why I didn't tell you right away," he responded, sounding exasperated. "Look, I am managing. Things are going fine, there is no need to get worked up."

"Dad. You can't tell me that she got lost in our own neighborhood and not expect me to be worried? When was this? And, how could she not know our address? You know that means it's getting worse. I can do more to help. Tell me what I should do?" I pleaded.

He paused for a few moments, looked at me, and then put his arm around me.

"Everything you are doing and have done is very good. We are always proud of you. Mom is happy when you come home, what, once or twice a month? That is all we need, Anu. I know you can't come home all the time, so please don't worry. You know I always tell you if I need something. Right?" he said, reassuring me.

I thought about this conversation often. He frequently tried to comfort me during difficult times, and thinking about his selflessness still made my eyes well up with tears. Those were the words I needed to hear.

While my work trips, romantic life, and social commitments kept me busy in D.C., my parents continued their usual routine, which was frequently complicated by my mom's growing memory loss and mental decline.

We headed into the grocery store and grabbed a cart. My mom was excited to be doing something on her own, to feel independent and useful. She was smiling again. Her smile has a way of warming you up inside. People are drawn to her when she's at her best.

I consulted her about which fruits and vegetables we should buy, doing my best to make her feel needed. I never realized how important all of this was, especially trying to keep her mind busy so that she stays alert. It's one of the many things I've learned over these past six years.

She placed the produce in our cart, then picked up more items that we already had at home—tea bags, salt, and whatever else caught her eye.

While she wandered off to pick more things, I hurried to take them out of the cart and place them out of her gaze. She caught me in the act, as I placed a bottle of ranch dressing back on the shelf. She began to whine, her voice growing louder and louder.

"What are you doing?" she shouted.

My patience started to wear thin. Then, my adult voice came out.

"That's enough! I told you how many times we have bottles of this at home. Finish those first," I said sternly.

I knew people were looking, but at this point, I was used to having a few stares. I couldn't afford to spend one hundred dollars during every grocery trip we went on. But, she tossed a bag of chips, a wooden spoon, and paper plates into the cart anyway.

"I want these!" she demanded.

At that moment, I gave up being so cheap. I knew this was really about her wanting to have some control.

"Fine, are we ready to go now?" I asked, returning to my normal tone. She nodded, triumphant. I exhaled again once we finally left.

By the time evening rolled around, my mom's home aide finally arrived.

"Thank goodness you are here, Fatimah," I warmly greeted her as she came in. Fatimah just smiled, taking off her coat and shoes by the front entry closet.

"I know. I know you are ready to get out of here," she laughed. "How is she today?"

"All over the place, but I think she's finally calmed down. She wants aloo paratha for dinner, and we still have some subzi in the fridge," I told her as if I was talking to a babysitter. "Oh, and make sure she takes her medicine tonight. Her sugar has been getting high the last couple of days. You know she can't control her bladder overnight when it gets like that."

⌒&

Thirty minutes later, I rushed down the steps wearing my black dress and leopard print heels, digging through my purse for the new lipstick I had just bought. My mom stared at me from the couch, inspecting my night-out look.

"Going to meet your friends? You should wear your red dress," she said, knowing my weekend routine.

"I'll wear it next time. You wanna come with me? Let's party!" I laughed, taking her hands into mine and waving them in the air playfully.

"No, I'm tired, but you go. Tell them I said hi," she said seriously.

"Make sure you take your medicine tonight, okay?"

"Okay," she said, sipping her chai.

These light exchanges are what makes the house we now live in feel like home. Whether I return at 1 a.m. on a Saturday night or at 6 p.m. during the work week, I know I'm not coming to a lonely, empty place. My mom's inquiries about my eating habits, her outfit recommendations, her eyes lighting up when I walk through the door—these moments will never get old for me, no matter how many tantrums she throws.

⌒&

Sometimes, I catch her looking at the framed black-and-white photo of her and my father on the bookshelf in the living room. They were a striking, well-dressed couple—dad in his checkered suit, sporting black-framed glasses and mom in a vibrant-striped saree, both smiling in front of a Gandhi statue in Delhi.

"That's my husband," she said to me while pointing at him. Then she looked at her younger self. "That's me."

She glanced up at me for some acknowledgment.

"You see my saree?" she paused. "I need more sarees."

Mom continued to look longingly at the photo, this time no smiles. With a tear running down my cheek, I stroke her hair.

"Yes, that's papa," I responded. "Mom, you look so beautiful." I put my arm around her and squeezed her tighter. "We can get you whatever you want, maybe a kurti or salwar instead? I'll find you some nice ones, with sparkles."

The photo reminds me of when the three of us were together on those weekend visits, where I observed the two of them closely. Whenever I tried to sleep in on Saturdays, I'd always wake up to footsteps outside my room, doors opened and closed, and the kitchen cabinets were slammed shut as my parents hustled and bustled around the house. In a groggy state, I would squint as I touched my phone to check the time—it was usually only 6 a.m., way too early to be up, in my opinion. I'd quickly turn over, irritated, and try to fall back asleep.

In the evenings, every once in a while, there would be arguments as we sat at the kitchen table.

"I don't need all these medications!" my mom would yell.

"You need to take them. Just take these and you are done, okay?" my dad would tell her as calmly as he could.

Every night like clockwork, my dad would bellow, "Leela, come, it's time for your insulin."

Mom would head to the living room on cue, where there was a small table by the couch with a glaring fluorescent bulb beaming from the table lamp. She would roll up her sleeve, as my dad got the insulin pen ready.

"Dad, how do you give her the insulin? Don't you need to write down how much she needs somewhere? Does it hurt her?" I asked one day. Most of the time, I never really paid much attention, but I wondered how he always knew what to do.

"It's not hard. If you do it properly, she doesn't usually feel it. But you don't need to worry about any of this. I'm taking care of it," he said in an attempt to dismiss further questions.

I wish I could still ask him these questions, but at thirty-four years old, the world fell on my shoulders, I was left to take care of my mother and had little time to grieve over the loss of the man who constantly told me not to worry.

What if I mess up? What if I do something wrong? What if she gets worse? These thoughts keep me up most nights.

But we keep going.

I set up the insulin pen, making sure I get the dosage just right.

"Mom, come downstairs. It's time for insulin."

DEAR MUTASSAN

BY RADHIKA MENON

MUTASSAN HAS PASSED AWAY, my dad texted me. The words just hung there.

I was working my first corporate job in New York City—miles away from my childhood home in Michigan and even farther from Mutassan, my grandfather, in Kerala—when I read these words and my world stopped turning.

At twenty-four, I was lucky to have lasted so long without losing someone I loved and too naive to anticipate the emotional toll of that loss.

A week before her father passed, my mom flew to India just in time. The journey across the ocean is exhausting when there is something to look forward to on the other side. It's even more taxing when your worst fears are unfolding at your destination. Halfway across the world, my mom sent infrequent but thorough status updates via WhatsApp, long paragraphs typed by tired hands. Later, she would tell us that a few days after she arrived, Mutassan woke up and saw her by his bedside. He lucidly asked about me, my brother, and my dad. Even then, family was on his mind. And then he slipped away.

Mutassan's illness began with a fall, which after a series of complications, led to long-term hospitalization. I never saw Mutassan while he was sick. I feel guilty for not having made the time to visit, but I am thankful that I only remember him as the vivacious, commanding person I knew him to be.

In my mind, he will always be the stern-looking man with salt-and-pepper hair perfectly parted on the right side of his head and an impeccably groomed pencil mustache, the man who would affectionately call me mole in Malayalam. My most vivid memory of Mutassan is the image of him in a short-sleeve button-down, waiting for us in the gleaming Kochi airport whenever we came to visit. Or maybe it is the sight of him swerving in and out of manic Indian traffic to buy the loaf of bread that I always requested for breakfast.

A few months before our grandfather's death, my mom had asked my brother and me to write Mutassan an email updating him on our jobs and our lives.

"Mutassan has been asking about you guys," she told me. "Just write an email. He'll be so happy."

My parents would remind me about this email every Sunday evening during our weekly catch-up call. I said that I would, just to get them off of my back. For months, I assured them that *this* would be the week I would send Mutassan a message. The weeks passed and I came up with more and more excuses, but I never wrote that email.

After my parents got married and my brother was born in India, my family moved to America, where I was born in the nineties. Our immigrant family maintained our connection to India with long-distance phone calls, blasting Hindi music in our home on weekend mornings, and frequent trips back home.

I dreaded those trips to India—not because I minded seeing my relatives or the lengthy journey, but because once we arrived, I was always bored. My American friends spent their summers on lavish cruise vacations and lying on beaches, and the last place I wanted to be was my grandparents' house with dial-up Internet and Windows 95. I hated the restlessness that enveloped me for weeks during those summers.

The last time I went to India was in 2009 after I graduated from high school, and I was especially ticked because of the number of graduation parties I had to miss just to visit my grandparents. This was the last summer that time was really mine, when vacation seemed to stretch on endlessly. That trip was like any other. My days were hijacked by family visits, and my nights were spent cursing the slow Internet that prevented me from logging onto AIM—the only way to reach my friends.

Occasionally, when the dial-up failed, I had to work up the courage to ask Mutassan to help me. I was nervous that he would judge me for my screen obsession. I floated through the trip with one foot out the door, so eager to return to my own life that I didn't bother to connect with the family members right in front of me.

It is only as an adult that I have begun to realize the strength of my parents, who left everything behind in search of fulfilling careers and a different life for their children. Only now do I truly appreciate my mom's sacrifice of parting with her parents to move to the other side of the world. My life's biggest move has been from Michigan to New York City after college, while my parents had moved eleven time zones away from the only life they knew. I never really thought about any of this before my grandfather's death. Even as my mom constantly reminded me and my brother to write those emails, I did not recognize the urgency of her pleas. I never fully understood the fact that these were *her* parents. That email to Mutassan meant as much to mom as it would have to him.

But instead of writing it, I did all sorts of inconsequential activities that seemed life-or-death in the moment—dating app swiping, boring dates borne from these swipes, hours of watching TV, and absentmindedly finding myself on social media while attempting to work on my creative projects. There was absolutely nothing keeping me from reaching out to my grandfather. I just never brought myself to do it.

After we got the news of Mutassan's death, I felt overcome by helplessness. Eight thousand miles away, my mom was having the worst day of her life, and all I could do was send her a WhatsApp message and hope that the WiFi would work. I briefly considered the possibility of attending the funeral until I realized that, even if I had left at the very moment I learned of my grandfather's death, I would never make it in time. I cursed the miles between us, and then the tears began.

I remembered when I decided to go to the University of Michigan, Mutassan looked it up online—on that never-upgraded dial-up Internet—and told me that it was a good school. After I graduated, he wanted to know more about my desire to be a writer and work in the arts. Instead of questioning me, he was supportive.

There are snippets of his existence that never leave me—the way he would emerge disheveled from an afternoon nap in a lungi and drink his tea in front of the TV, carefully pouring a measured amount from the teacup into the saucer and slurping every last drop. He would talk back to the TV no matter what he was watching, whether it was a tennis match, the local news, or the Indian cricket team. He'd insist on driving himself everywhere, even in that awful traffic, and was stubborn about letting go of that bit of independence when his eyesight began to fail.

I've spent hours thinking about the email I would send him if I still had time:

Dear Mutassan,

I'm doing well. Actually, I'm doing more than well, living in a city that encourages me to live fully and chase the dreams that you always supported. I feel so grateful to be pursuing creative things.

I came to India for your first death anniversary puja, and I wish it had been you waiting for us in the bright white Kochi airport, ready to stuff our overpacked suitcases into the trunk of an Ambassador cab. I always thought that I would see you again, and I feel mountains of remorse for not prioritizing family the way you always did.

If I've learned anything, it's that life is short. The things you take for granted will slip like sand through your fingers before you even realize they're gone. I promise that I will never forget this lesson, but I wish I had learned it under different circumstances. I hope that you can forgive me for not sending this sooner, and I hope that you are still proud of me.

Your Mole

The following story contains sensitive material that may
be triggering for trauma survivors and those who suffer
from mental health conditions. Suicide and murder are
some of the topics mentioned in this author's moment.

If you feel triggered, please know there are resources to support you.

U.S. National Suicide Hotline
1-800-273-8255

KIRBY JACKSON

BY RAKSHA MUTHUKUMAR

IT WAS A WEDNESDAY NIGHT, and I was at my friend Yamini's campus apartment. We were sitting with our friends on uncomfortable dorm couches and playing music a little too loud. We had a few drinks while we decided if we wanted to stay in or go out. My phone rang, and the name Kirby Jackson flashed on the caller ID. I stepped out because I never miss a call from my best friend.

While I expected to hear Kirby's voice on the other end of the phone, her mother's called out to me instead. Angela Jackson sounded matter-of-fact and a little distracted, the way I imagined she sounded when talking to her students as a dean at Emory University.

"Hi, Raksha, how are you? I'm calling to let you know that Kirby shot herself tonight. I found her when I came home. I'm going through her recent contacts to inform people. Take care, good night."

I asked some inane questions as the news slowly penetrated the fuzz that had developed in my mind. *Did she kill herself?*

"Was she successful?" I inquired, hoping I heard wrong. "Where did she get the gun?"

We later learned she had it for more than a year without anyone knowing. She bought it at a trade fair outside Atlanta.

After hanging up with Angela, I had no idea what to do next. I stood in the hallway, listening to the music from the apartment. I couldn't just leave without saying anything to Yamini. I couldn't go home and face my roommates, who also loved Kirby. I couldn't break down in the middle of the hallway. I settled on helping Kirby's mother make her series of nightmarish calls. I broke the news to my friends, Simeon and Kate.

"Thank you," they said.

"Yeah, of course."

Eventually, I had enough of the hallway, and I knocked on the door. Yamini quickly dismissed the party. It was easier than I expected. Something in my expression must have warned everyone away. I felt awkward telling Yamini what happened to Kirby, and I worried about being an imposition on a school night.

But she held me as my tears finally came. She called my hall director, while I spoke to the head of LGBT Center. I cried as they watched me silently. No one knew what to say.

Kirby was a Black transgender woman who died at the age of twenty-four. She loved trains. She loved the rain. She liked puzzles and worldbuilding. We shared similar complexions that allowed us to wear makeup with names like mocha and caramel. She had a medium-length afro and wide eyes under her distinct eyebrows. Her eyebrows made her easily identifiable even in baby photos, with their almost-horned peaks on the outside and stuttering gaps on the inside. She had a big laugh that made her entire face scrunch up.

To have even one friendship in life like my friendship with Kirby was a privilege. If you've had one like it, you understand. We ate Taco Bell in our pajamas and talked about how she'd be a bridesmaid at all my weddings—I suspected our friendship would last longer than any marriage I fell into. We teased each other about our predictable taste in boys and girls. We imagined the trouble we'd still get into as old ladies. We always took each other's side against everyone else in the friend group. If there were things we didn't tell each other, I don't remember them.

Kirby was also always suicidal. It was a defining characteristic of friendship with her—heart-stopping late-night calls, philosophical debates about the inherent value of life, visits to rehab where she was held after an attempt. My freshman year boyfriend and I had a no-phones-in-bed rule—except for Kirby, of course. I used my resident adviser privileges more than once for midnight check-ins after friends called me worried about her. There were belts, there were pills, and finally, there was a gun.

Georgia Institute of Technology did not have any professional LGBT resources until 2015, leaving us students with the responsibility of holding therapeutic office hours and late-night vigils for one another. Without a system to support us, we didn't get to clock out. I spent my late teens and early twenties in a chronic state of anxiety without knowing there was any other way to be. Only years later did I recognize that a nineteen-year-old should not have been talking her friends down from ledges every weekend.

My friendship with Kirby was worth it. Describing how she paid me back is easy—she loved me unconditionally. I didn't have to be smarter or less smart than I was. I didn't have to be less slutty and more sober. I didn't have to be more slutty and less sober. Her candor about her own demons made it easier to confide in her about my own. I didn't have to pretend that I didn't sometimes question the point of it all because Kirby would never judge the thoughts in the darkest corners of my mind. She taught me her politics and how to imagine a kinder and more just world, but she was also the one who taught me to parallel park and curl my eyelashes.

When my girlfriend and I broke up after an idyllic summer of planning our lives together, I was beyond devastated. I felt outside of my body, and I was afraid of what I might do if I was left alone. Kirby was the only person who could coax me out of it. I lay on my bed and asked Kirby to speak in endless monologues to stave off my panic attacks. Kirby rubbed circles on my back till I fell asleep, then grabbed a pillow and slept on the floor near my bed.

The first time Georgia Tech punished Kirby for existing was her eviction from campus housing for a suicide attempt. The next was when they arrested and banned her from campus for protesting the police-shooting death of our friend and president of Pride Alliance, Scout Shultz.

The fall semester of 2017 opened with the public execution of Scout on September 16. Student-captured cell phone videos, that feel burned into my mind, showed a student outside of the west campus dorms on a lamp-lit street, engaging with Georgia Tech police officer Tyler Beck. Scout brandished a multitool and approached Officer Beck. There was a gunshot, and then Cat, Scout's best friend, ran screaming toward their body.

Campus police officers were supposed to protect students—it's their core responsibility. Scout was experiencing a mental health crisis and posed no threat to anyone except themself. I keep trying to imagine my friend—a skinny, nerdy youth who loved to play *Dungeons and Dragons*—appearing scary enough that they were deemed fit to kill. I cannot.

In the aftermath of Scout's murder, the campus body spoke up valiantly in defense of Officer Tyler Beck. Emails from the school's administration called for unity as one Georgia Tech family. Smear campaigns appeared on the Georgia Tech subreddit and in Atlanta newspapers, all of which adamantly misgendered Scout by refusing to use they/them pronouns. Students hung "We Stand with GTPD" signs in their dorm room windows. I remember doing my rounds as a resident advisor and wondering if my neighbors would have hung the same signs after my own death.

Two nights after the shooting, students and faculty held a candlelight vigil at the Georgia Tech campanile. Around 500 people gathered to remember Scout's visionary leadership and their quirky spirit. Scout had served as the campus Pride Alliance president for two years and many students remembered them as the face of queer Georgia Tech—even if they didn't know Scout personally. We mourned, and we silently asked ourselves what we could have done differently. I remember fervently wishing I was more involved with the Pride Alliance and helped to lessen the burden on Scout's shoulders.

Toward the end, the tone of the vigil changed. Transgender students cried out against the institutions that ignored their mental health. Protestors gathered on the edges of the crowd and began handing out flyers calling for a march. Our grief held a deep sadness but also vast rage. The flames were fanned, and the crowd marched to Georgia Tech Police Department headquarters.

"You murdered one of us!" Kirby yelled during the protest.

She tried to protect her friends—Cat in particular. Cat was

arrested, screaming "Fuck you—you killed my best friend!" as she was placed in the back seat of a police cruiser.

Kirby came home with a broken umbrella and a broken heart after watching her friends tormented on a night that was supposed to bring healing. Georgia Tech police showed us once again that our pain was not going to be tolerated.

Kirby saw Cat as a younger version of herself, a young Black transgender woman who she sought to mentor and protect. In the weeks after Scout's death, Kirby joined a group of friends who rotated the responsibilities of keeping Cat company and making sure she was fed and rested.

One of my strongest memories during this time was when I texted Kirby, telling her that she should take care of herself instead of giving away all of her energy. She texted me back, `Scout was Cat's best friend. Think of how you'd feel if it was me.`

Several days later, Kirby received a court summons regarding her participation in the protest. Georgia Tech President Bud Peterson had called for all demonstrators to be identified using cell phone footage. It seemed as though he wanted to ensure that the grieving students were suitably punished. Kirby texted me saying she was going in and would not have her phone. She told me not to worry, but I worried anyway. She spent a night in Fulton County Jail and was then banned from campus, effectively banished from all of her friends.

"Do you think she'd like this one?" Angela asked me.

"I'm sure she would," I replied, looking at the urn.

I felt sick because I actually wasn't sure. I couldn't remember Kirby's favorite flower, and I had forgotten her favorite color. Her mother and I looked at each other anxiously, attempting to piece together the girl we loved from our fragmented memories.

On December 14, there was a funeral at All Saints Episcopal Church, where I gave the eulogy. I wrote it between my psychology and algorithms exams that morning. It was my first funeral at a church, and I felt conspicuous in my black sweater under the golden altar. I sat in the back row until Reverend Kim Jackson called for me. I looked out into the crowd and saw rows of black outfits and straight backs. I made eye contact with Kirby's mother and grandmother as I spoke.

At the end of my speech, I left the room before my knees gave out. I fell to the floor and wailed. I felt disgusting sitting on the ground alone despite the room full of mourners who could probably hear my sobs. I wanted someone to come to me. I didn't want anyone to come to me. I wanted Kirby to come to me.

At the reception that followed, we ate cheese and fruit while looking at photos of Kirby and sharing stories of her. My friends smiled at me sadly, and I, in turn, smiled at Kirby's grandmother sadly. It was horribly uncomfortable.

By the time it was polite to leave, it was dark outside. It was unseasonably cold for Atlanta, even in December. I prefer the warmth, but Kirby would have thought it was a nice night out. I watched my breath form small clouds as I walked home.

Permanently etched on my right shoulder blade is a cloud raining on a pair of joined hands. The hands form a pinky promise shared between two best friends.

I *won't forget you*, one says.

I'm *always with you*, says the other.

SOMEDAY, MAYBE

BY NEHA PATEL

THE BIG FAT INDIAN WEDDING. Five words that conjure up images of a week filled with festivities leading to family bonding and memories. Each moment is filled with laughter and joy, captured in zillions of photographs snapped by guests—but what the pictures don't show is what lies beneath the smiles. They don't show the cultural and societal expectations placed upon the bride, groom, and their respective families. They don't show the stress these expectations cause. In my family, the bulk of this stress lies squarely upon the shoulders of women. Depending on their role in the family, each woman feels the strain of their unique obligations from the moment the wedding preparations begin.

It has been nineteen years since my big fat Indian wedding. At twenty-six years old and only one year out of college, my husband and I told our parents about our relationship. We left out the fact that we had dated for four years and let them believe we had only just met. Our parents were overjoyed, wedding planning started immediately, and it was straight to the mandap for us.

Being American-born means making compromises, such as

keeping my dating life a secret. These compromises were made to try to bridge the gap between what I felt was right for my life versus what my family and the Indian community deemed appropriate. After all that time, I now realize these compromises have chipped away at my sense of self.

All of these thoughts swam around my mind and drowned out my sons' voices as they argued over a game on their iPads. It was Memorial Day weekend, and we had flown into humid Atlanta, Georgia, for the wedding festivities of one of my husband's cousins. It was a three-day traditional Gujarati wedding extravaganza, and tonight was the final event—the reception. I tried to quiet the boys down with a stern look and went back to precisely folding the pleats of my sari and tucking them into my petticoat. I sighed as I looked into the mirror, wishing I had tailored my sari blouse to be sleeveless.

"Do not wear sleeveless! It is not appropriate for a married woman to wear that type of design," my mother-in-law warned in a succession of phone calls during the weeks before the wedding.

The calls started out with the normal logistical planning:

"When will you be getting to the wedding? Which hotel will you be staying at?"

But, as the wedding neared, each subsequent call became more intrusive. The questions turned into directives.

Eventually, my mother-in-law stopped suggesting what I should wear over a phone call and would FaceTime me instead. She made a show of squinting behind her bifocals and moving her face dramatically close to the screen while making comments about my weight as she vetoed my outfit choices.

"Your face is looking a bit rounder since the last time I saw you, beta. Are you exercising? You know that even walking thirty minutes per day is good for your sarir," she said.

I opened and closed my mouth. No sound came out.

"Also, you should not eat out so much. You should cook more often. Extra weight causes you to look so much older."

Instead of trying to defend myself, I nodded.

She immediately smiled, taking my nod as a sign her assumptions regarding my lack of cooking were correct. She continued down her list of reminders.

"Remember your mangalsutra, okay?"

"Mummy, I have already packed my jewelry, including my mangalsutra," I shot back.

As we discussed the jewelry pieces I had packed, I recalled that day nineteen years ago when my husband and I had traveled to New York to shop for our wedding. My mother-in-law, along with her two sisters, had accompanied us into an Indian jewelry store in Jackson Heights, home to the neighborhood known as Little India. Being a minimalist with jewelry, I had my heart set on a mangalsutra with a tiny pendant. My mother-in-law had an entirely different vision.

"Na. Na. Na. Absolutely no. We cannot buy that small mangalsutra. What will everyone say when he puts it on you in the mandap? Go over to the other showcase by the cash register. We'll ask the uncle to show us the bigger mangalsutras over there. We'll find the perfect one."

We left the store with a mangalsutra that satisfied her and all of the people who would potentially try to find things to gossip about at a wedding. I had wanted to wear a tiny mangalsutra on a daily basis, but the jumbo, medallion-sized, 22k, gold pendant attached to the one she bought did not make that an option. It was a constant reminder of her not listening to my opinions—to this day, whenever I put it on for an event, my memories transport me back to that store in Jackson Heights where I felt invisible.

We finished our FaceTime session, and I felt defeated as I ended the call. Days later, I was still replaying the image of my smug mother-in-law's face on loop. My internal voice criticized me for not keeping my reaction in check. After all, it was not the first time she had insulted my weight or started a conversation with niceties only to begin criticizing and then insulting me. It was not the first time she felt the need to control me. Being an optimist, I hoped she would change, but I was only a fool who was always surprised when she came in for the kill. Our saas-bahu drama was alive and well, with the bahu not voicing her opinions in order to maintain the peace, yet never being able to please her saas.

I finished applying my favorite lipstick as I tried to push away the memory of the phone call from the week before. Taking a look at myself in the mirror, I noticed the smile plastered on my face. It was not a smile that reached my eyes. It did not exude joy. It was the smile of a puppet. I was a marionette who was performing on stage while my mother-in-law pulled the strings.

Her son, on the other hand, was never subjected to her demands. He was just expected to be himself. He was only told to be clean-shaven, and even that instruction had fallen to the wayside as he had taken on a cross between a goatee and beard. One look at him on the first day of the wedding festivities and my mother-in-law had blamed his unshaven face on me.

"Do you really like the hair on his face?" she asked. All eyes on me, waiting for my response, I knew she was willing me to say no. I desperately looked from my husband back to her.

"Mummy, he likes it, and I think it looks good," I said.

"I don't like it. It doesn't suit him. You should tell him to shave it off," she said through pursed lips before turning her back to smile at her son.

I was expected to sit, talk, and dress properly, tend to all of the elders, know what was going on in each of their lives, and ask them appropriate questions. In other words, I was supposed to know my place. My husband would speak about his career as a doctor, and the entire family would be enamored by his every accomplishment. Yet, no one asked me about my career or interests outside of the kids and our household.

Powdering my nose one last time, I thought, Not once has my mother-in-law shown an interest in my career aspirations, passions, or advocacy work. In the earlier years, I would begin a conversation about a situation at work, and she would absent-mindedly reply, "Uh-huh, okay, beta."

She would then interrupt me and change the conversation:

"Have you started to cook today? It would make me so happy for you to show an interest in learning his favorite dishes. I can even teach you." Or, "You know when you fold his laundry, it would be helpful if you rubberband his matching socks together. He is so busy, and this would make it easier for him in the morning. I used to fold his socks like this when he was in school."

In her eyes, my goals did not pertain to her aspiration of me taking care of her son. I was supposed to be a supporting actor in the production of our marriage, while he was the lead.

I know my husband has never expected the same things as his mother. However, he has also never intervened with his mom on my behalf. At the beginning of our marriage, I would ask if he could gently speak up for me. I wanted him to respectfully let his mother know that a good wife can take care of her husband and the household while maintaining her own identity. He said nothing and explained that I needed to pick my battles, and in his opinion, this was not a battle that could be won.

As I gathered up the strewn-out cosmetics on the hotel desk and placed them carefully back into my makeup bag, I allowed my empathy to seep in. My mother-in-law had a college degree in teaching. She had worked for about three years in India prior to getting married in 1967. After her marriage, she had moved into her in-laws' home as was tradition, never working in her chosen profession again. My older sister-in-law was born shortly after, followed by another daughter, and then my husband. Immigrating to London and then to the United States only left my mother-in-law with the option to follow her husband's career and care for her children. Her story allowed me to think that perhaps she just doesn't know better. She treated me as her mother-in-law treated her and as generations of mothers-in-law have treated their daughters-in-law. Did it justify her actions? I had thought so for nineteen years. But as time wore on, her criticisms and judgments increased, and I was no longer inclined to make excuses for her.

As my thoughts wandered down this dismal rabbit hole, my husband emerged from our hotel bathroom, steam following him from the hot shower. He smiled at me and let out a whistle.

"Wow. You look beautiful."

At this, I genuinely smiled back at him. I knew in my heart that he has always respected my intellect, passions, and drive. He has always supported me wholeheartedly in any new endeavor I wished to pursue. So why do I need to have my mother-in-law's support? Why did I feel such a strong desire to make her understand my perspective and value me as more than a cleaning-cooking-child-rearing-husband-worshipping daughter-in-law? Why was it so important for me to be truly seen by her?

Deep down I knew *why*. By becoming who she wanted me to be, I felt as if I was slowly being erased. I wanted her to know that who I am matters.

I shook my head to clear my thoughts. *We are in Atlanta for a wedding, for God's sake. No time for a pity party.* I walked over to the closet and handed my husband his black suit with the tie and shirt I had carefully picked out the week before. I finished combing the boys' hair, turned off the iPads despite their protests, and hurried them out of the room to head down to the reception.

In the lobby, the boys rushed to push the elevator button as each of us stood in front of the door we thought would come to our floor first. It was a game we played as a family since the boys were toddlers. We dissolved into laughter as the doors in front of me opened, declaring I was the winner. We piled into the elevator, and the butterflies in the pit of my stomach started swarming. I began to sweat and realized that I was about to break. Not in a meltdown, nervous sort of way—rather in an epiphanic, Oprah "Aha!" moment kind of way.

As the opening elevator doors thrust us into the lobby filled with English and Gujarati chatter, appetizer plates piled high with aromatic samosas and chutneys, and brightly colored sarees and sherwanis, I did not see a blur of commotion. For the first time, there was clarity. There would be no change in my mother-in-law's perspective. The change, no matter how difficult and uncomfortable, would have to come from me. Was I willing to take whatever consequences that entailed?

I nodded politely and greeted those I knew with a "Tame kem cho?" As I approached the table numbers, my mother-in-law appeared at my elbow, grabbing my arm, and pulling me to the side. She was wearing an intricately embroidered black sari and heavily adorned with her best gold jewelry. Understated was not in my mother-in-law's vocabulary. As she smiled at other guests walking by us, she spoke in a rapid-fire Gujarati whisper into my ear:

"Why didn't you call Masaji when he got home from the hospital after his gall bladder surgery? Lata Masi's daughter-in-law called him in the hospital and then again when he was discharged home. He just told me now that you did not call after he came home. I told you to call immediately. Did you call?"

She continued to pleasantly acknowledge other aunties and uncles who walked by as she waited for my response. I felt a humiliated warmth rise up from my chest and move up my neck, extending to my cheeks reaching all the way to my forehead. I could feel the sting of tears in my eyes and I willed my voice to remain calm. Almost forty-five years old, and there I was being reprimanded for embarrassing my mother-in-law in a tone and manner usually reserved for a toddler who had misbehaved. Before I could answer, she repeated her question with more urgency and fierceness.

"Did you call? This looks so bad. Why would you not call?"

"Mummy, I did call. I called on the day you told me the news," I responded. "I spoke with Masaji for a few minutes while he was in the hospital. He was doing good, and they were keeping him overnight as a precaution because of his fever. I had left a message on his voice mail the day he was discharged."

"Why didn't you call back after you left the message and speak with him personally?"

And that was my grave error. Between work, end-of-school-year chaos, and packing for the wedding, I had forgotten to make my follow-up phone call. My daughter-in-law scorecard was now lower than the other daughters-in-law in the family. How dare I embarrass my mother-in-law?

"When you go into the hall, the first thing you do is go to Masaji's table and explain that you left a message and you are sorry for not calling back. Ask how he is doing and make sure you let him know that if he has any medical questions, he can call you guys. Okay? Did you hear me?"

I nodded. She gave me one last stern look, turned to the reception doors, beckoning for my oblivious husband, sons, and father-in-law to follow her. She was now all smiles as she entered the hall, leaving me outside to regain my composure. I took a deep breath, straightened the pallu of my sari, and walked calmly into the reception hall. As I entered, my eyes found the bar to my left and my husband waving from our table toward the right. I made a beeline for the bar and ordered two glasses of wine, red for my husband and white for me. I then proceeded to Masaji's table, where my mother-in-law was within earshot, sat down in the empty seat next to him, and asked him how he was doing and how the surgery went.

"Masaji, you look so good. When I called you in the hospital, you said you were doing good but feeling a bit of pain. I checked with masi on all of the medications prescribed to you, and they are correct."

"Thank you, beta. I am just finding it hard to eat a lot right now. And I am still tired," he said. "I didn't get the proper chance to talk to you earlier because I left early yesterday and this morning from the lagna because I was so tired."

"It will take time to get back to normal," I reassured him. "Just be patient. You are doing better now than when you were in the hospital. It will take a couple of more weeks for your body to get back to where it was. Call me anytime if you have any more questions. Okay?"

Masaji nodded and smiled. I excused myself to go sit at my table, giving my mother-in-law a tight smile. I did not apologize for not calling him back. I listened to him with genuine concern. And, I was confident from my mother-in-law's expression, she would be sure to tell me later that I should have said I was sorry. As I stood up, I saw that my mother-in-law had taken her seat at the adjacent table and was pointedly staring at the wine glasses in my hands.

I passed by her on my way to my table, remembering how she had not wanted a bar at our wedding. She had gone so far as to insult my family by stating that "bars may be the norm in Patel weddings, but at Jain weddings, we do not engage in such sinful behavior." She had gotten her way, and there had been no alcohol served at our wedding. Little did she know that her son, along with all of the groomsmen, had toasted the night away at the hotel restaurant bar right outside our reception before hitting the dance floor. I quietly chuckled at the memory.

I sat down at our table and made a show of placing one wine glass in front of my husband and the second in front of my plate. The brilliant light from the myriad of chandeliers in the ballroom caught the rims of the wine glasses. They sparkled and became the focus of the table. I raised my eyes to meet my mother-in-law's as she nervously laughed with the other relatives seated at her table. She furtively glanced about, hoping no one had noticed the wine glasses in front of our plates. I could guess exactly what she was thinking. How could she possibly explain her daughter-in-law drinking to others when she had declared her own beliefs in Jainism to include the strict adherence to the prohibition of alcohol? I picked my glass up, bent toward my husband, and clinked my glass with his. As I brought my glass to my lips, I held my mother-in-law's gaze. I raised one eyebrow and took a long satisfying sip as her eyes widened with disbelief. Placing my glass down on the table, I sat back in my chair as the evening's speeches and entertainment began.

Would I be getting a call from her tomorrow? Yes.

Would I defend myself? No.

There was nothing to defend. There was no explanation needed. There was no approval needed. I will not be defined by her definition of sanskar.

After dinner, the guests began to make their way to the four long dessert buffet tables. I joined the line with my boys, helping them load their plates with gulab jamuns, chocolate-covered fruits, and petite cakes. I was sure they would dance the sugar away before crashing to sleep. I made a plate for my husband and me to share, as well as another for my mother-in-law, noticing she had not moved from her seat.

"Sweetie, before you go to your table, please go give this plate to Dadima. Be sure to tell her we grabbed the last couple of chocolate-covered strawberries for her. You know how much she loves those," I said to my older son.

Both boys headed in the direction of my mother-in-law's table as I made my way back to my husband. His eyes widened with delight as he took in the desserts I had brought back. As we dug in and enjoyed the richness of the cassata wedding cake, my mother-in-law appeared at our table.

"Mom, you doing good? Enjoying yourself? How did you like the food?" my husband asked.

She nodded and smiled.

"Everything was very good. The sweets were so delicious. The boys brought me a plate of chocolate-covered strawberries and told me, 'We got the last couple for you, Dadima.' I didn't know that they knew I liked those." She laughed lovingly and looked over at me knowingly.

It was a peace offering of sorts—not a concession but a show of sanskar. I could only hope this evening was a baby step for the bahu in our drama to find her voice and the saas to listen. Someday, maybe, she will finally listen.

AMOR INDOCUMENTADO

BY SABINA ENGLAND

ONE DAY, WHILE SCROLLING ON SOCIAL MEDIA, his pictures caught my attention. I was drawn to his genuine smile and twinkling eyes. I messaged him, and to my delight, Alberto wrote back. I gave him my number. He texted me and we chatted in Spanglish.

How are you? I typed, unable to think of anything else to say.

I'm so feliz, he texted back.

Feliz? Why are you happy? I asked.

Because I am talking to you, he replied. I blushed. He was already a charmer. Where you want to eat? I wanna take you out.

No sé. I like to eat everything, I replied shyly, unsure of how to respond. I was suddenly conscious of coming across bossy or demanding.

Mmm. How about Indian food? I will pay. You are a queen, and I wanna treat you like one.

I remember blushing and feeling incredulous. Was he serious?

Lol hell no. I'm Indian, remember? I eat Indian food every day at home and I'm sick of it, I texted back.

I sound like a bitch, I thought to myself, worried he would think I was negative, rude, and entitled.

How about Mexican? he texted back, seemingly unfazed.

Sure.

He picked a Mexican restaurant near downtown. I wore a pink floral print dress. *The date will be a bust,* I thought to myself, preparing for the worst, *but I'll look cute anyway.* At the restaurant, Alberto approached me with a single rose.

"Gracias," I muttered, flustered. "Hey, look, this flower and my dress match. Same color!"

"Sí," he said, smiling and nodding. "Same color. Very pretty."

I was not used to lipreading a heavy Mexican accent, and he had difficulty understanding my deaf intonation. Alberto was in the first steps of learning English, and I knew a little Spanish but not enough to easily carry a conversation. I showed him signs in American Sign Language. He enthusiastically copied me, repeating hand signs with a huge grin plastered across his face. We used the Memo app on our phones to communicate faster.

He asked me what I would like to order. I scanned the menu for the cheapest option, not wanting him to spend too much on me. I decided I'd have two tacos.

"Muy bien," he said and suggested I try the maíz tortillas.

"¿Maíz? ¿Por qué?" I asked.

He took out his phone and typed in the Memo app.

In Veracruz, we make maíz tortillas. No wheat. People in North Mexico eat wheat. Maíz taste more better than wheat. I think you will like.

I was taken by his charm and attracted to his gentle soul and his long black hair tied in braids. His smile hooked me, and by the second date, I already felt comfortable with him. He was different from other men I went out with in the past. My heart was strung around by the others who saw me as a fling—an exotic, deaf, brown thing to date for fun and then discard. Some of them were immature and too impatient to learn how to communicate with a deaf girl. I was exhausted by dating.

I had always been an angry lone wolf, the punk girl. I didn't have many friends. People mocked my speech. I felt disconnected from my family for being the only deaf person in the entire clan. And, I didn't feel accepted or welcomed around South Asians, Muslims, deaf people, or white, hearing punks.

My speech skills weren't perfect and people didn't always understand me, which left me feeling inadequate and embarrassed. My sign language skills were subpar. I had attended a deaf-oral school that taught lipreading and verbal speaking, but I didn't speak confidently. I used American Sign Language, but I terribly lagged behind other deafies who signed better, smoother, and faster.

What I excelled at was filmmaking, writing, and performing onstage. By the time I met Alberto, I had written and directed my first narrative short film, which premiered at Tribeca Cinemas in New York City. I was proud of my accomplishments, but I was desperately lonely. I wanted to share my success with someone. I wanted to love and be loved.

And as Alberto and I got to know each other, my rage dwindled. All of my anxiety disappeared when I was with him. He gave me a safe space to truly be myself. I didn't have to worry about speaking with my voice or try to change myself to appear more desirable. I respected how he appreciated everything in the world. I loved that he loved life. I was learning to be happy and let go.

Alberto taught me to admire the beauty in the world. He was

a joyous presence, lighting up any space he entered. He loved working and eagerly seized any opportunity to help out. He worked in construction, laying brick and tuckpointing. Having grown up in a shack without running water in a small village, Alberto was grateful for any job he was hired to do. He rarely got mad and almost never complained.

As our relationship bloomed, Alberto began to reclaim his indigenous Mexican heritage. Indigenous people in Mexico are like the Dalits—the Untouchables of Mexican society. They are discriminated against and looked down upon by the rest of the country. Alberto had been ashamed of his roots back home in Veracruz, but after crossing the border and meeting many people in the United States, he became energized by indigenous movements that fought for justice and celebrated native culture and identity. I empathized. Being Indian, Bihari, Muslim and fully deaf, I also felt embarrassed of my background until I learned more about my culture.

Alberto told me that his father was Huastec Nahua and his mother was Totonaca. The Totonaca are said to have built the El Tajin pyramids, an ancient site in the tiny yet bustling city of Papantla near the Gulf Coast. Alberto said they were known for smiling—their predecessors, the Remojadas, even created happy smiling figurines. Alberto, like his mother, was born with a smile on his face despite having lived a life of hardship and being discriminated against by others due to his background.

I found out about Alberto's undocumented status on a sunny day in early autumn. We were en route to a food festival downtown. As the train hurtled toward the city square, I proposed we travel to Washington D.C., where I was booked for a performance. I suggested we take the Amtrak and view the countryside.

Alberto looked sad. He wistfully responded that it was not

possible to take the train. I asked him why, and he replied that he didn't have papers. He said that people working on Amtrak were known for reporting brown people and calling ICE. He knew some folks who were seized, jailed, and deported by agents after boarding the train.

"That's awful," I murmured, shaking my head in disbelief.

"I know," he said. "Sabina, do you still like me?"

I looked at him, my mouth agape.

"What? Of course, I still like you. I want to be with you and spend my life with you," I blurted out.

He looked relieved and smiled again. That night, we held hands and watched the bands performing onstage. Alberto wanted me to enjoy the music despite my deafness, so he told me the name of each song that played. He never got annoyed with me for pestering him. He was patient.

We talked about our future together. Everything was uncertain. Alberto didn't know if he would be able to stay in the country. I worried about how my parents would react to our relationship because he was not Muslim or desi. I worried they would be judgmental about his undocumented status and the fact that he was poor. While we were dating, I was overjoyed when I spent time with him but anxious about what was to come. Did we have a chance? Was I wasting my time?

One day, I texted him about making plans to meet and got no response. I became concerned, thinking he was no longer interested in me. The next day, I received a message on Facebook from a mutual acquaintance of ours:

Alberto was picked up by ICE agents yesterday and is being held in county jail. He will be transferred into federal custody and put on trial for illegally crossing the border.

My heart dropped.

I visited the jail almost every day to see him. His knees hurt badly. He was demoralized. He felt ashamed and loathed himself. It was heart-wrenching to see him in such a bad state. I tried to cheer him up and stay positive, but I wanted to scream.

I realized that I loved him. Hell, I was madly, hopelessly in love with him. The thought of being separated from him made me feel violently ill. How could we be together when he was being deported back to his home country? I tried to resign myself to the fact that we would be forced to part, but I just couldn't.

My parents noticed my erratic behavior and asked me what was wrong. I refused to speak until one day I broke down and told them the truth. To my surprise, my father was sympathetic. He even went to visit Alberto in jail and introduced himself.

Later, he asked me if I had feelings for Alberto.

"Yes. Are you mad at me, Abu?" I replied, my heart beating fast.

"No, I'm not mad." he said. "Sometimes it just happens. Are you happy with him? Is he a good man?"

"He's the best, Abu," I replied. "Wallahi. He is a very good man. One of the best people I have met in my life."

"Yes, I can see that," he responded. "When I met him, I could sense what a good person he was."

I was shocked and relieved by his positive response.

"You are my daughter," he continued. "If you want to go to Mexico and be with him, you have my blessing. I want you to be happy."

"Wow. Thank you, Abu," I said, lost for words. Feeling emboldened by my parents' support, I persisted, hopeful that Alberto and I would find a way to be together.

I went to Alberto's trial. It outraged me to see him in shackles like a murderer. I wanted to tell off the judge, bailiff, and guards for being unkind to meri jaan. The judge ordered his deportation back to Mexico and permanently banned him from re-entering the United States. Alberto would never be allowed to step foot on American soil again.

After he was deported, we made plans to be with each other. We were reunited in Mexico City, and he took me to Veracruz to meet his family. None of them spoke English, but they welcomed me. They knew I was deaf, so they used writing and texting to communicate with me in Spanish. The kids even called me tía. I felt completely at home.

Mexico felt strangely familiar to me. It was like India—colorful, bursting with energy, a place where tradition and spirituality were valued. People respected their elders and families were considered sacred. They prayed to saints and performed songs and dances in the streets. Mango trees grew everywhere, just like back home in Bihar.

Most importantly, I found home with Alberto. I knew how extremely fortunate we were, unlike thousands of families broken up by deportations and left unable to see each other.

Our love grew and we flourished together. I gave him pieces of traditional Indian clothing. He read the Qur'an, prayed salaah, and took the Shahada at a masjid in Mexico City. I learned some Nahuatl and wore a huipil to honor his heritage. He braided my hair and put flowers in it. We thought we would spend forever together.

I lost my beautiful Alberto in a car accident three years ago. When I received the news about his death, I collapsed. I was completely destroyed. Half of my soul was ripped out. When I saw his lifeless body, I almost fainted. I crumpled into a chair. His sisters were astonished. They said his face changed as soon as I stepped into the house to see his body. They told me he had been expressionless, but that his lips curled into a smile when I rushed over to his side because he needed me there to be with him.

For two days during the wake, I sat by him, looking after his body and speaking to him. I didn't want to be away from my jaan. He was mine—I would make sure his body was safe. I sensed his presence in the room. He was gone, but his soul was still there. I knew he could see and hear me. I felt his sorrow and shock. He couldn't believe he was dead either.

My eyes became puffy from crying non-stop. I was furious with Allah. Nonetheless, I arranged my Alberto's funeral because it was important to me that he move to the light in the afterlife and rest in peace. I did not want his soul to agonize over me or his family.

Alberto's parents and I buried him in a lime tree grove on top of a lush, green mountain overlooking a river. It was the perfect resting place for him, a lover of nature.

A year and a half after his passing, I created a solo show with sign language, music, dance, and poetry, which premiered in Arizona. On the opening night, as I performed on stage, I looked into the audience and there I saw him. Despite being blinded by the bright spotlight, I glimpsed a faint outline of a man with two black braids. After the performance, I frantically looked around, searching for him. No one else had seen him. I then wondered if it was Alberto in spirit, watching over me for my first performance.

I think of him every day. I pray and I ask Allah to bless Alberto's soul, to help him be happy and free in the other world. I imagine him as an ethereal being with his love flowing through my body. I speak to him, and I know that he hears me.

ACKNOWLEDGMENTS

THANK YOU TO Trisha Sakhuja-Walia, CEO of *Brown Girl Magazine*, for giving us the space, time, and support to pursue this labor of love. Without your leadership, energy, and trust, we would have never been able to bring this project from the idea stage to the bookshelf.

Thank you to Mango & Marigold Press, especially Sailaja Joshi, for believing in our mission and choosing *untold* as your first-ever book for adults. Your support and guidance have been invaluable, appreciated, and needed.

Thank you to Tanuja Desai Hidier for writing a foreword that captures the spirit of this book and for being one of our very first readers. Your energy and excitement helped us to continue to keep the midnight oil burning during the final editing stages.

Thank you to Mitali Desai, our copy editor, who pored over each of these stories with us and provided insightful feedback to our contributors that helped them hone their pieces into their final form.

Thank you to Aishwarya Sukesh for creating the beautiful cover art. You compiled the ideas that were nothing but words before you came along and brought all of our—sometimes conflicting—visions to life with grace and professionalism.

Thank you to Simran Sarin for designing the subtheme artwork. Your illustrations helped us envision what this project would look like in its most early stages.

Thank you to the hundreds of people who responded to our open call and were willing to share their most personal moments with us.

And to the courageous individuals who allowed us to help them tell their stories in this book, thank you for being so willing to dig deeper. Even when it was hard and uncomfortable. Even when you had to confront moments that were deeply personal and, at many times, traumatic. Even when life got busy and a pandemic changed the world as we know it. Thank you for never giving up. Your stories pushed us forward and inspired us. It has been an honor to work with you.

Lastly, thank you to our friends and family who gave us constant support, endless amounts of food, and an empathetic ear when we needed it. Without you, we would not have been able to see this dream through.

With love and gratitude,
Gabrielle & Kamini

CONTRIBUTORS

SAAHIL sees themself as a writer and intercultural educator who has learned the importance of storytelling first as a student in the classroom and later as an educator. They speak Spanish and Portuguese and hope to learn Hindi and Arabic. They are currently pursuing a graduate degree in anthropology and education at Teachers College in New York City. They tend to write about love, lust, and longing—particularly where these notions intersect with the fine lines between optimism and pessimism, joy and melancholy, innocence, and insight. Saahil hopes their work diversifies existing literature and elevates historically oppressed voices as they continue to publish more in the (near) future.

NOVA A. is a Bangladeshi-American model, actress, creative, activist, and Knicks Poetry Scholarship recipient. They often use their platform to discuss LGBTQ issues, diverse representation in media, as well as speak out against rape culture. Nova made their acting debut in an Off-Broadway documentary theatre piece called *Sharum*. You may recognize them from several music videos from artists such as Yung Baby Tate and Ali Gatie and in campaigns for brands like WeSoForeign by Anik Khan.

M.K. ANSARI is a Canadian-born Silicon Valley Fortune 500 corporate lawyer, television writer, and mom. She has written for prominent outlets including Reuters, CNN, and *The Huffington Post* and is a former editor of *Illume Magazine*. She currently works as a lawyer and is also writing for two pre-production stage streaming programs while pursuing the Professional Program in TV Writing at UCLA. She is the co-founder of the Muslim Women's Art Society and co-host of The *Good Girl Playbook Podcast*, a podcast about brown women who defy cultural norms.

JESSIE BRAR is a public speaker, writer, and mental health activist from Toronto. Growing up, she struggled a lot with her own mental health, and in an attempt to understand herself more, she went on to study psychology at Queen's University. After graduation, Jessie found there was no space for South Asians to have safe mental health conversations and started *The Mental Health Spotlight*. Jessie was recognized as one of the Top 100 Most Influential Sikhs Under 30 in 2020 for her work in this space. She continues to further these conversations through her podcast *Presents of Mind* and by sharing her story at events around the world.

NUPUR CHAUDHARY is an urbanist, strategist, ceramicist, and dreamer based in New York City. She loves gardening, exploring cities, and getting to know dogs of all shapes and sizes. She can be reached at www.nupurchaudhury.com

SHIMUL CHOWDHURY is a Muslim Bangladeshi-American artist currently residing in Central Florida. She received a BFA in art and technology from the University of Florida and an MFA in digital arts and new media from the University of California, Santa Cruz.

Her recent work aims to record and share the lived experiences of Muslims in the U.S. through textile craft, dialogue, and participation. Outside of her art practice, she is also passionate about teaching, playing video games, and knitting.

CHANDRA COATS is a transracial adoptee originally from Kolkata, West Bengal, and raised in Southern California. She is now a stay-at-home parent but has done advocacy work for children, sexual assault survivors, and immigrants. She is married to her husband, Dan, a friend since childhood. She is of a confessional Reformed Christian faith and is a political independent.

SABINA ENGLAND is an award-winning filmmaker and playwright whose works have been shown in London, New York City, Los Angeles, Paris, and other cities around the world. She recently wrote, produced, and performed a solo show called "Allah Earth: The Cycle of Life" at New York International Fringe Festival. She recently won a Jury Award in Los Angeles for her short film, *Deaf Brown Gurl.*

MEERA SOLANKI ESTRADA is the host and producer of *kultur'D*, a pop culture radio show on Global News Radio in Canada. She is also the founder of FUSIA Media, a premiere online destination and experiential hub for the modern Canadian South Asian Woman. It is where fashion, lifestyle, and entertainment intersect with global citizenship. A wife, mother, and media maven, Meera wants to inspire women to live their best life in the pursuit of their passions and goals. She has bylines in *ELLE Canada, Shondaland, Bustle, The Huffington Post, CBC Life, FLARE,* and *Chatelaine* to name a few. She also appears regularly on local and national television and radio broadcasts as a beauty and culture expert. With a degree from the Schulich School of

Business paired with a post-graduate in radio and television broadcast journalism, Meera's education and experience are a force of media savvy. She embodies her brand mantra of fashion meets compassion South Asian style.

RAJVIR GILL is a lawyer currently working in the area of children's rights. Before law school, Rajvir completed her bachelor's of commerce (because her dad said it was the practical thing to do) and earned a master's in political science (because she wanted to). She worked in the not-for-profit sector in her hometown of Edmonton, Canada, where she led projects against gender-based violence and human trafficking. Outside of her work and being in school for a very long time, Rajvir has interned and studied in many places around the world, igniting not only her passion for travel but also her desire to work in human rights and international law. Books and stories have always been a constant companion for her, giving her access to other worlds. Therefore, Rajvir's contribution to this project is the realization of a life-long dream to write and share the difficulties of her life in order to connect and provide solace to others who may need it.

L.M. IYER (pen name) is a graduate student studying creative writing. She grew up in a small coastal town but currently resides in the American South. Her work revolves around themes of perception, identity, and transition.

RAVLEEN K. is a marketer and writer based in Austin, Texas. Having lived her life between five cities in various regions of the country, she uses her diverse experiences to advocate for mental health awareness with MannMukti and write thoughtful pieces on religion and culture for *Brown Girl Magazine*. Drawing on her love for Punjabi music, she also serves as an editor for brwncltr.com. Ravleen works in marketing full-time in the tech industry.

DURIBA KHAN is a Texas-based writer and student with work published across a spectrum of digital media. Her interests include improv, filmmaking, reading, pursuing the most cinnamon-y chai latte in the greater Austin area, and studying the law.

J. LALWANI is a first-generation Indian American. She works as a stockbroker and recently completed her master's degree from Harvard University. She has interests in women's empowerment, racial inequity, and self-discovery. She is an avid runner and loves a good joke.

NINA MALAGI, born and raised in London, works and raises her tribe in NJ.

RADHIKA MENON is a pop culture-obsessed writer whose work has appeared in *Teen Vogue*, *Decider*, *Paste Magazine*, and *Brown Girl Magazine*. She is a proud alumna of the University of Michigan, is one-half of the comedic video duo PromRad, and is a self-professed pizza enthusiast. She resides in New York City.

RAKSHA MUTHUKUMAR is a Southerner-turned-New Yorker with a deep love of brunch, beer, and books. She is a podcaster and writer who believes in storytelling as a means of empowerment for the marginalized. Raksha is passionate about the radical liberation of all people, and she is actively engaged in queer activism and work at the intersection of social justice and technology. By day, she is a software engineer at Google.

AMRISA NIRANJAN is a Guyanese-born artist and muralist who creates work to engage audiences in dialogue about the nuanced contemporary immigrant and minority experience. The focus of her work is further elaborating the narrative of the world's colonized diaspora by identifying often overlooked collective aspects that stitch descendants of once-colonized or once-enslaved people to one another. Niranjan highlights the enigmatic beauty of these cultures, which evolved to transcend histories of trauma to create multitudes of new expression in music, art, dance, and languages that continue to impact the world today.

KIMBERLY PAREKH has a distinguished career in working to provide equitable access to education in developing countries. On the side, she has taught at the university level and is a fierce breast cancer patient advocate. She lives a healthy and active life, despite living with advanced disease through the love and support of her close family and friends and collaborative health professionals, as well as many integrative and holistic health approaches.

NEHA PATEL is a fiction and creative nonfiction writer. Born and raised in Ohio, she currently resides in Texas. She graduated with a degree in pharmacy from The Ohio State University in 1999. She is an advocate and 2019 graduate of the Texas Partners in Policy Making program. Her short story in this anthology is her first publication.

POOJA PATEL is a former economic developer from Atlanta, Georgia, who is married to her high school sweetheart. After years of infertility, miscarriage, and infant loss, she shares her story so others know they are not alone in their struggles. Pooja's passions include community development and women's reproductive rights.

RADHIKA PATEL is from Leicester, U.K. but lives and works in London for a social justice campaigns organization. She believes the world would be a better place if everyone engaged with their power and privilege more, got messy eating mangoes over the sink more, and shared food with loved ones more.

PRIYAL SAKHUJA is currently a fourth-year medical student who is passionate about preventative medicine and women's health. She is in the pursuit of using her medical career to work with underserved communities. In her free time, Priyal loves to spend time with her family and friends, binge-watch Netflix, read, and travel.

SHARDA SEKARAN is a Michigan-born, New York City-raised, global wanderer. She writes fiction, essays, and articles on topics such as identity, culture, music, human rights, race, drug policy, and travel. As a veteran communications professional and consultant, Sharda has been a figure behind major social issues, such as criminal justice reform, marijuana legalization, health care as a human right, and LGBT equality. She was a 2016 VONA/Voices Fiction Fellow, where she studied under acclaimed author Tayari Jones. Sharda is a great believer in the empathic and transformative power of stories. She is working on her first novel and is currently based in Copenhagen, Denmark.

RITA SENGUPTA is a queer South Asian-American actor and comedian based in Brooklyn, New York. Her work has been featured by WNYC, *Buzzfeed*, and *Glamour Magazine*. The most recent festivals she's performed at include NYC Sketchfest and Asian Comedy Festival. You can find her around NYC doing stand-up and performing with various sketch comedy groups. Rita studied at Atlantic Theater Acting

School and Upright Citizens Brigade. She graduated from Washington University in St. Louis with a BSBA in finance and marketing.

NISHA SINGH is an NGO professional in Washington, D.C., with a focus on women's rights and empowerment and citizen engagement. She is currently pursuing a part-time master's in public policy at Georgetown University. Her hobbies and social media content include pursuits of structured fun, such as book clubbing, volunteering with Sister District DC, and teaching a weekly Doonya: The Bollywood Workout class.

SUBRINA SINGH holds a bachelor's degree in Asian and Asian American studies from Stony Brook University and a master's degree in South Asian religion and philosophy from Columbia University. She is a contributing author in the anthology of Sikh love stories, *Her Name is Kaur*. Since its release, she has become committed to using her experience with mental illness to help better the mental health awareness within the South Asian community. Subrina was a featured guest on TV Asia's Shades of Shakti and has collaborated with organizations such as SAMHAJ NAMI and NYC Department of Mental Health and Hygiene. She is proud of her journey and determined to use her own experience with bipolar disorder to help others suffering with mental illness.

ANANTHA SUDHAKAR is an associate professor of Asian American studies at San Francisco State University, where she teaches courses on Asian American literature and South Asian American history and culture. Her writing has appeared in *The Scholar and Feminist Online*, *The Journal of Cancer Education*, *Small Axe*, and *The Asian Pacific American Journal*, among others. Prior to her teaching career, Sudhakar spent a decade as an arts organizer in New York City. She currently serves as an academic advisor for the South Asian American Digital Archive, the largest historical repository about South Asian American immigration.

APOORVA VERGHESE, born in England and raised in America, considers herself a modern-day nomad. As a student at Tulane University, she hopes to further her knowledge on culture, identity, and its effect on this world. In the future, she hopes to pursue a career in civil rights law.

HENA WADHWA is a women's activist and former educator who earned her doctorate at Florida State University. Her research interests stem across women's health, motherhood, mental health, and maternal and child health. Hena pursued her career as a special education teacher (aka "intervention queen") and taught in neighborhoods that were underserved and lacked appropriate resources for students with disabilities. After serving a few years in education, Hena discovered that across educational realms, there was a particular emphasis on mothers, their roles, and expectations. She is determined to utilize her research and leadership to bring forward the voices and experiences of all women and, in particular, highlight the experiences of South Asian American women. She is excited to pursue a career that embodies research, advocacy, and leadership. Hena is the first woman in her family to pursue and accomplish a PhD and is dedicated to her mission of women's rights and equality. Besides striving to do right by women, she also loves kickboxing, weightlifting, herbal teas, and watching reruns of *The Golden Girls* (her spirit animal is Sophia and Dorothy—confirmed by a *BuzzFeed* quiz).

ANITA WADHWANI received her master's in public and international affairs from the University of Pittsburgh and her bachelor's in journalism and mass communications from Point Park College. During her graduate studies, she was an intern at the Department of State and has made a career working in policy and government in Washington, D.C. Outside of her career, Anita has advocated for mental health awareness and elderly care in the South Asian American community, due to experiences within her own family. She was named a 40 Under 40 honoree for leadership in 2018 for Northern Virginia. Anita enjoys writing to express herself and is an avid reader of *Brown Girl Magazine*.

ABOUT THE EDITORS

GABRIELLE DEONATH is a Guyanese-American writer, editor, and content creator based in New York. She hopes to give voice to those without a platform and promote authentic representations of minorities and marginalized communities through storytelling. Her writing has appeared in publications including SISTERS *Magazine*, the Muslim Creative Writers Network anthology *Survival of the Hardworking*, VirtualMosque.com, and *Brown Girl Magazine*, where she has also served as an assistant editor for the Indo-Caribbean and political teams. Read more of her work at www.hijabdiaries.com.

KAMINI RAMDEEN is a Guyanese-American editor, graphic design artist, photographer, and small business owner based in New York City. She previously managed editorial teams at *Brown Girl Magazine*, where she led political and Indo-Caribbean coverage. She is the founder of Paulo Grand, a streetwear apparel company that seeks to create awareness and spark conversations about the first-generation American identity and its many intricacies.

ABOUT THE TEAM

TANUJA DESAI HIDIER is an author/singer-songwriter. Her pioneering debut *Born Confused*, considered to be the first South Asian American YA novel, was named an American Library Association Best Book for Young Adults and was hailed by *Entertainment Weekly*, *Rolling Stone Magazine*, and *Paste* as one of the greatest YA novels of all time. Sequel *Bombay Blues* received the South Asia Book Award. Tanuja's album *When We Were Twins* (based on *Born Confused*) was featured in *Wired* (as the first booktrack). Music video "Heptanesia" (from her booktrack album *Bombay Spleen*) was a BuzzPick on rotation at MTV Indies. Tanuja also produced the *Deep Blue She* music video/PSA: an award-winning intersectionality project featuring over 100 artists and activists. She is working on her next book and album. Visit ThisIsTanuja.com to learn more.

TRISHA SAKHUJA-WALIA is a digital content creator and social media strategist with a knack for event planning. She manages more than 200 contributors, oversees business development and on-going marketing initiatives at BrownGirlMagazine.com and SlashieConnects. co. She thrives off her slashie lifestyle, has a passion for publishing meaningful content, and is always on the hunt for the next big story.

After years of not feeling accepted, she's proud of her hyphenated identity and is on a mission to find unique ways to empower South Asian womxn living in the diaspora. Raised as an Indian-American in the suburbs by immigrant parents, she resides with her husband in New York City.

AISHWARYA SUKESH is a journalist and artist whose work is inspired by game changers in the South Asian community living in the diaspora. Through an intersectional lens, she uses illustration, graphic design, and other skills to help elevate purpose-driven messages and brands. She can be followed on Instagram @aishwarya_sukesh.

SIMRAN SARIN is a senior at UC Berkeley studying Interdisciplinary Studies with an emphasis on Precision Healthcare & AI. Her academic interests range from healthcare to technology and equity. She loves traveling, live music, trying new food, and of course, art. Her artwork revolves around identity in the context of the South Asian diaspora and is a way to indulge in a world unbound by preconceived notions of race and ethnicity.

MITALI DESAI is a writer and editor based in New York City. Her work can be found in *Kajal Magazine*, *4x4 Magazine* and the *Columbia Current*. She is a founding editor and writer at *Half Sour Magazine*, a digital literary journal.

BROWN GIRL MAGAZINE, born out of the lack of minority representation in mainstream media, was created by and for South Asian womxn, who believe in the power of storytelling as a vehicle for community building and empowerment. Through diverse, multimedia content and community building, *Brown Girl Magazine* empowers and engages those who identify as a part of the South Asian diaspora with a hyphenated identity. With CEO Trisha Sakhuja-Walia's lead and vision, alongside a passionate team of more than 200 freelancers, BrownGirlMagazine.com continues to serve as an anchor for South Asians by remaining steadfast in publishing premium, multimedia content to uplift, create deeper understanding and connection, and cultivate meaningful dialogue in communities around the globe. In addition to publishing their first-ever anthology, they've released a podcast, *The Chaat Room*, launched SlashieConnects.co, a new-age community elevating those with creative passions, and produced an apparel line, Ladki Power.

MANGO & MARIGOLD PRESS is an award-winning independent publishing house that shares the sweet and savory stories of the South Asian experience. Sharing everyday and extraordinary stories of the South Asian experience, the company has produced fifteen books across four different product categories with features on *The Today Show, The New York Times, The Washington Post, US Weekly, People Magazine,* and so many more. *untold: defining moments of the uprooted* is the company's sixteenth book and first young adult anthology.